"Perhaps it took a global pandemic. If anyone had doubted that being a pastor was a challenging calling, the events since early 2020 have demonstrated what Fred Lehr so passionately addresses in the revised and expanded edition of his book *Clergy Burnout*. In easy-to-read yet profound chapters filled with practical examples from his long experience in the field, Lehr leads us from pain and depression to healing and hope. In the process, he shows the way to renewal and restoration after the long haul of a horrific pandemic. As he himself says, 'It's time to center our lives in the Gospel.' Good news, indeed!"

—Wolfgang D. Herz-Lane, former bishop,
Delaware-Maryland Synod, ELCA;
senior pastor, Christ the King Lutheran Church,
Cary, North Carolina

"Fred Lehr's work on clergy burnout brings together a wide range of necessary topics for active clergy. The core of his work is restoring pastors by exploring codependence and personality types, but he goes much further. He also focuses on hope and healing and provides a practical guide for transforming how we think about our work in congregations. In addition, Lehr's concepts have been immensely helpful for training lay pastors. His work on developing spiritual maturity is particularly critical in the mainline church today, when we need leaders with depth, knowledge, and biblical literacy."

—Jill Peters, director, Crossroads Lay Leadership Program,
Moravian Theological Seminary, Bethlehem, Pennsylvania,
and author of *Missional Blueprint*

"Fred Lehr has proved once again that he has a pulse on the continuing challenges of clergy burnout. This revised and expanded edition includes many new insights into clergy burnout from a psychological perspective, such as pastoral and congregational codependencies and how to treat them, and particularly, how to move from codependence toward the healthier alternative of interdependence. I found Lehr's focus on spirituality and his 'Spiritual Life Survey' particularly helpful. Clergy and congregations alike will find *Clergy Burnout* a valuable tool for these challenging times for communities of faith."

—Ron Reaves, retired ELCA pastor
and author of *The Rector's New Dawn*

CLERGY BURNOUT

OTHER BOOKS BY FRED LEHR

Becoming a 21st-Century Church: A Transformational Manual. Eugene, OR: Wipf & Stock, 2017.
This book provides practical and experience-based ideas to appropriately respond to our shifting culture while keeping a strong emphasis on the gospel of Jesus.

Power Currency: How to Grow, Enhance, and Stop Squandering Your Personal Power. Ashland, VA: Rand-Smith, 2020.
In the midst of turbulence, we can feel quite powerless. But when we properly manage our personal power—mental, emotional, and spiritual—it will grow.

CLERGY BURNOUT

Surviving in Turbulent Times

REVISED AND EXPANDED

Fred Lehr

Fortress Press
Minneapolis

CLERGY BURNOUT
Surviving in Turbulent Times, Revised and Expanded

Scripture quotations are from the New Revised Standard Version Bible © 1989
Division of Christian Education of the National Council of the Churches of
Christ in the United States of America. Used by permission.

Spiritual Life Survey Copyright ©1982 John Fred Lehr, revised 2006.

Cover Image: schankz/Shutterstock.com
Cover Design: Brad Norr Design

Print ISBN: 978-1-5064-7430-4
eBook ISBN: 978-1-5064-7431-1

CONTENTS

PART TWO
HOPE AND HEALING

PREFACE TO THE REVISED AND EXPANDED EDITION

IT'S TIME

I served a congregation in Northern Vermont. Yes, lots of winter there, but beautiful. During the vacancy before I arrived, the congregation was near insolvency. Leaders would count the Sunday morning offering, look at all the unpaid bills, and decide if they could remain in operation one more week. I discovered that only after I arrived.

A few years later, it became evident that we needed to expand the building. There were too many children for the nursery during worship and for the available Sunday school space. Plus, a real office was needed. So we embarked on a three-year, step-by-step venture to determine the way forward. A study task force was organized that reported to the full congregation regularly. After each report, permission was granted to take the next step and report again. At the end of the three years, it became evident that a new addition, doubling the size of the building, was the solution.

How could we convince the congregation, so recently barely able to pay its bills, to now embark on a serious building project? Someone needed to make the pitch. Who would be our "closer"? We picked a leader I'll call Bob. Bob was the kind of guy who thoroughly reflected on anything before he said it. As a result, when Bob spoke, he was almost always dead-on. He would nail it. And we all trusted what Bob said because he was so careful in his pronouncements. Thus Bob was chosen to give the speech before the congregation about the new building project.

In his standard, brief manner, Bob said, "It's time." That's it.

Actually, he did say a few more words, but he began with "It's time." And we all knew it.

The same is true for this second edition of *Clergy Burnout*. It's time.

We are facing a huge shift in our culture. Phyllis Tickle, in her book *The Great Emergence*, documents that Christianity goes through a major cultural shift every five hundred years.[1] Well, it's been five hundred years since the Reformation. It's time for a major cultural shift. As if that weren't enough, people in the United States and many places around the world are dealing with a pandemic, an economic crisis, serious cultural and social movements such as Black Lives Matter and LGBTQIA+ and gender equality efforts, climate change, and more. These are all important challenges and worthy of our attention.

The pandemic alone is enough to send our world, including the world of congregational ministry, into a dither. It's late 2020 as I write this new preface, and we still don't know if, when, or how we will be able to worship again in our church buildings as we did before—with singing, handshakes, and all the rest. How do we practice ministry—making hospital calls, home and shut-in visits, and much more? Committee meetings and choir practices have been set aside or are being done through online platforms. The pandemic has upset everything and made the work of a church professional all the more difficult.

The reason for a second edition of this book is that while nothing has changed dramatically with regard to the issues enumerated in the first, many new social realities have emerged.

Over the decades, the respect given to those of us who serve in church leadership positions has not significantly improved. Similarly, compensation is still not commensurate with our level of education. According to a Duke University study, "The national data show that average clergy earnings remain below the earnings of similarly educated workers, and clergy have lost earnings ground in recent decades when compared to the average earnings of other full-time, salaried, graduate educated workers."[2]

The issues identified in the first edition have not changed because they are so deeply embedded in the DNA of the church. The church evolves very slowly. (That's a whole problem on its own.) But now, in the twenty-first century, in light of some new social realities, there is a cry for change. We can respond to that cry and facilitate wholesome, healing innovation.

It's time! It's time to champion clergy wellness and well-being.

It's time to dive deeply into issues such as establishing and maintaining healthy boundaries in ministry and regaining life balance—physically, spiritually, emotionally, professionally.

It's time to better understand the realities of codependence in ministry and all the pressures and problematic behaviors and attitudes codependence causes.

It's time to examine spiritual maturity and invest in its development.

Most of all, it's time to center our lives in the gospel of Jesus Christ—good news, hope, unconditional love, and an open future.

It's time!

So please investigate thoroughly the topics in this new edition. For those who have read the first edition, it's time for a review and for renewed dedication to healthy ministry and the themes here presented. For those new to *Clergy Burnout*, it's time to begin practicing ministry in sound and more appropriate ways that lead to a rewarding life and years of faithful service to our Lord.

It's time! God bless!

ACKNOWLEDGMENTS

Many authors save their families for last in the acknowledgments. I want to start with my wife, Janet, who endures all my craziness and yet still loves me. She is far more than my spouse; she is my greatest supporter and my best friend. My son and my daughter are two of the most engaging and neat people I have ever met. They are an inspiration to me. I adore my son-in-law, my grandchildren, and my great-grandchildren. They are such a blessing.

I also owe profound gratitude to my staff at the Church Renewal Center at Good Shepherd Rehabilitation Hospital in Allentown, Pennsylvania. Together we did some marvelous work helping church professionals regain balance in their lives—spiritually, emotionally, physically, and professionally. This was one of the finest clinical teams ever assembled. We saved lives—and careers and more. Our eight years together were not nearly enough.

Gratitude must also be expressed to the thousands of pastors and other church leaders I have encountered across the nation as I led workshops and seminars. The latest count is about five thousand such dedicated people who have heard me speak or accepted my counsel and direction.

I am indebted to Anne Wilson Schaef and Diane Fassel for their excellent book *The Addictive Organization* and other writings; they have provided many of the insights reflected in this work. In addition, the Myers-Briggs Type Indicator (MBTI) published by the Consulting Psychologists Press in Palo Alto, California, has had a dynamic impact on the development of this project. All references to the MBTI reflect this important connection.

The wisdom of Donald Hands, PhD, gave me a framework that was essential to a complete understanding. The codependency graph was his original idea.

Many thanks to Loren B. Mead, who suggested the brief research project included in this work. The wider church has been blessed by Loren's contributions through the Alban Institute.

And to the many, many others who touched my life with their tender support, who encouraged my exploration, honored my struggles, and stand by me yet—I thank you with all my heart.

Part One

PASTORS IN PAIN

1
PAINFUL PASTORING

Every denomination has annual judicatory meetings where pastors and lay leaders gather to carry out the business of the church. Among Lutherans like myself, these gatherings are called synod assemblies. Yet one such assembly, which I remember quite well, came to be known as the "Pain Assembly." During the course of our meetings, pastor after pastor went to the microphone and expressed "pain" in the practice of ministry. That is to say, the very practice of parish ministry had become painful for them. And these were not the unsophisticated rookies; they were mostly the seasoned veterans of our church. But they were also veterans of a struggle to find a way to serve the church without all that pain, a pain of which they lacked any significant understanding as to its source or its course. This parade of suffering clergy was asking for help: Could someone—anyone—help them find relief?

For eight years, I watched another parade of pastors in pain come through the Church Renewal Center, a specialized treatment program designed exclusively for church professionals, at Good Shepherd Rehabilitation Hospital in Allentown, Pennsylvania. All these pastors were engaged in an all-too-familiar struggle: to serve faithfully without losing their minds, their families, and even their souls. It was a struggle I knew well from my own thirty-plus years in ministry, most of that spent in a local parish. Over time, I came to recognize that what got these clergy rewarded in their ministries was also the very thing that was wrecking their personal, spiritual, and family lives. After all, congregations love those who just can't say no. Congregations applaud those who never take a day off, who "labor for the Lord" endlessly. What heroes and heroines they are! How we admire their dedication! Or is it their disease?

SIGNS OF TROUBLE

The signs of trouble among our clergy have been with us for some time and show no indication of abating. A study conducted by Fuller Theological Seminary in the late 1980s uncovered the following:

90 percent of pastors work more than 46 hours per week.

80 percent believe that pastoral ministry is affecting their families negatively.

33 percent say that "Being in ministry is clearly a hazard to my family."

75 percent have reported a significant crisis due to stress at least once in their ministry.

50 percent felt unable to meet the needs of the ministry.

90 percent felt they were not adequately trained to cope with the ministry demands placed upon them.

40 percent reported at least one serious conflict with at least one parishioner at least once a month.

70 percent of pastors do not have someone they would consider a close friend.

37 percent admitted having been involved in inappropriate sexual behavior with someone in their congregation.

70 percent have a lower self-image after they have been in pastoral ministry than when they started.[1]

In 1994, Michael Lowe Morris and Priscilla White Blanton published an article entitled "The Influence of Work-Related Stressors on Clergy Husbands and Their Wives," in which they stated,

Clergy rank in the top 10 percent of the population in terms of education, but rank 325th out of 432 occupations in terms of salary.

Clergy families lack adequate quality time together, thus eroding family identity and cohesion.

Boundary ambiguity by the clergy family system produces problematic concerns regarding privacy and triangulation.

Clergy are described as being in the "holy crossfire," as the clergyperson and his/her family attempt to juggle the expectations of self, family, congregation, denomination, and God.[2]

More recently, a national survey of more than 2,500 religious leaders conducted in 2001 by Pulpit and Pew, a research project on pastoral leadership based at Duke Divinity School, found that 10 percent of those surveyed reported being depressed—about the same as the general population—while 40 percent said they were depressed at times or worn out "some or most of the time." This study also discovered other serious health problems among these leaders, including the astounding statistic that 76 percent of clergy were either overweight or obese compared to 61 percent of the general population. These findings were supported by a survey of Lutheran ministers that reported that 68 percent were overweight or obese, while 16 percent of male pastors and 24 percent of female pastors complained of problems with depression. Evangelical Lutheran Church in America data indicate that 75 percent of clergy work more than fifty hours per week.[3]

All of this does not exceed my own experience. In my thirty years of parish ministry, I had a terrible time saying no to my parishioners. I loved it when they needed me. After all, I was there to do God's work; how could I turn them down? Or so I told myself. In reality, it exhausted me, and I hated constantly being caught between my family and my congregation. I found myself falling helplessly into what we call burnout. Nevertheless, I pushed and pushed to be the perfect pastor. I kept annual statistics. Each year had to be better than the one before. More home calls, more hospital calls, more pastoral counseling—I was driven. At no time could I declare, "This is enough." I had no concept of "enough." Of course, I could not control how many people got sick and went to the hospital. Nor could I control how many people came for pastoral counseling. But I kept pushing just the same. Do more. Be more. Be that perfect pastor. Someday, you just might make it.

CLERGY BURNOUT: A SCENARIO

Perhaps a brief scenario—in which I depict a church professional who represents a compilation derived from clients I knew at the Church Renewal Center as well as other clergy colleagues—will paint a more complete picture of a pastor hurtling headlong into burnout. It is at once no one particular person's story, yet it is nearly *every* pastor's story:

It's morning. Early morning. Too early in the morning. I must rise and face the day. Yes, I know, Lord, "This is the day the Lord has made, let us rejoice and be glad in it . . ." and all of that. Tell you what, Lord: *you* rejoice in it and then fill me in later. I'm going back to bed.

No, I'm not. Just kidding. Got to rise. *Oh Lord, help me make it through the day.* What will this day have in store for me? And will my to-do list ever get done?

The kids. Are they up yet? Are they getting ready for school? And my dear wife, what a blessing she is. How is she doing with her morning preparations? Off to work she goes. Kiss her good-bye. Tell her I love her. God be with her.

Get the kids fed and ready for school. The bus is coming. Kiss them good-bye. Tell them I love them. God be with them.

Now for me. Shall I take the time to exercise? I really ought to exercise—my blood pressure and my cholesterol and all. But if I take the time for that, then I will get to the office later, and I've just too much to do today. So I'll just skip the exercising today. Like too many days. I ought to take better care of myself. Maybe tomorrow? Washed. Shaved. Dressed. Quick breakfast. Not nutritious, but it will do. Off to the church early, before people know I'm there. I've got to start work on Sunday's sermon. And then there's my column for the newsletter—overdue! The secretary will be on my back for that. And she should be. My tardiness only throws her off schedule. So I better get that done.

Email. How many emails? Twenty? Oh no—do I take the time to deal with all of that? And the mail, now piled high on my desk; if I don't go through at least some of that, it will suffocate me. Hope I can get some of this done before the phone rings. Too late. They found me. Hello. Oh, Mabel, how are you? Oh my, the hospital? How is your husband? Surgery? Okay. What time? When do they expect him out of recovery? This afternoon? I'll be by for sure. See you later. Mabel, you and Henry are in my prayers. Take care. Any time. Bye.

Lord, look after Henry and Mabel. They need your help.

Let's see, now, where was I? Yes, Jane. Yes, I know. The newsletter. I'll get to it today. I promise.

Lord, help me get to the newsletter!

George, how are you? Good to see you. Interrupting me? No, that's fine. Come in. What can I do for you?

The kids in the gym—yes. Now what? Broke what? Not again. Well, I guess we'll just have to fix it. George, what can I do? If we don't let them in the gym, then they'll just be out on the streets and get into trouble. I know. We need more supervision for the kids while they're in the gym. I'm working on it, George. In the meantime, let's just do our best. Okay? Thanks for stopping by. Any time.

Newsletter! *[phone]* Hello. Helen, how are you? The yard sale this weekend—yes. What? Not enough volunteers. That's a problem. What do you want to do? You want me to call people and recruit more volunteers? Okay, I can do that. How many more do you need? Ten?! Really? How about three? Can you make it if I get you three more volunteers? Good. I'll do my best. Thanks for calling. Any time. Bye.

Newsletter! Lord, what do I say? I've probably said it all a long time ago. What do they need to hear that they haven't already heard a dozen times? How can I make it fresh and new after all these years? It's that same, wonderful message—our hope is in the Lord. How many ways can I say that? *Lord, have mercy . . .*

Hey, John *[the sexton]*! George says there's a mess in the gym. Can you go and check it out? George may need some help. And cool it on the kids always breaking something. Tell George we're doing our best. Okay? Thanks.

Newsletter!! Maybe I'll work on the sermon for a while? It may inspire me. What are the lessons for this Sunday? Oh no, not those again—fire and damnation. I can't say all that negative, judgmental stuff from the pulpit; it only upsets the people. They always want a kind and gentle message that will lift their spirits and make them feel good. Who wants to hear about their sinfulness? They need to hear that. You can't cure what you refuse to diagnose. If we won't face our sins, we'll never overcome them. But if I tell it to them straight, I'll only get complaints. Been there, done that, no thanks. So what will I do with these texts? Maybe I'll do the newsletter now instead.

Newsletter!! Let's see . . . *[phone]* Hello. Jim, how's it going? Yes. The youth group. The retreat in a few weeks, yes. Not enough youth have signed up. Well, you know they always wait till the last minute. But you need to plan the meals and the transportation. I know, it's a problem. What can I do? Can I call all the families and encourage the youth to come? Gee, can't you do that? More will come if I call them? I see your point. I guess so. What's your deadline? Next Sunday. Okay, I'll try to call all the families by next Sunday. Thanks. Any time. Bye.

Volunteers for the yard sale. Youth for the retreat. Time, Lord.

I need more time.

What, Jane? The newsletter. Yeah, sure, almost done. *[I lie.]*

Newsletter!! Well, I'll talk about our Sunday school and how proud I am of our teachers who give so much of themselves to the children. That's always a winner. But I did that just three months ago. Can't do that again already. Maybe the altar guild. That's it. I'll write a big thank-you for the good work of the altar guild.

Here, Jane. My column for the newsletter. Yes, I know, it's late. And that throws you off your schedule. Sorry. I'll try to do better. *[phone]* Hello. Betty, how are you? Your mother? What's up?

She fell. Again? How is she? Where is she? At home. Well, I'll try to stop by and see her. Is there a good time of day? This afternoon. Sure. Tell her I'll be there. Okay. Thanks. Any time. Bye.

What time is it? Noon already? Where did the morning go? Let's see, got to see Henry in the hospital. That's across town.

John is in the hospital too. But that's a different hospital. So I need to swing by there. Then there's Betty's mom. Where do they live? Oh, way out there. Oh well, got to go.

What time do the kids get home from school? Got to try to get all these visits in before the kids get home. I hate it when no parent is there to greet them and they're home all alone. They're good kids, but it's just not fair to them. Got to do better.

And there are our shut-ins. Can I squeeze in a visit to one of them while I'm out? Who haven't I seen lately?

Tonight I have the stewardship committee meeting. What do I need to prepare for that? And tomorrow is the Bible study class. Got to get that ready too. I guess I'll just have to skip the shut-in visit for today. Too much to do.

But I hate myself when I ignore the shut-ins. They can't get out and be among people. They really appreciate my visits. They need that human interaction to keep them going. I feel guilty when I put them off. But what else can I do?

Well, I'd better get going. Maybe I'll skip lunch? No, too hungry. I guess it's fast food again. There goes the cholesterol and the blood pressure. Lord, you've got to help me here. I can't do it all.

Home late in the afternoon. Apologize to the kids that I wasn't there when they got home. Apologize to my wife that I have to eat and run. Stewardship meeting, and I'm not prepared. Phone calls—got to make phone calls. Yes, I know. Do it better. I'll try.

Lord, you've got to help me. I'm doing my best, working long hours, denying my own self-care, abandoning my family, failing to pay attention to my dear wife, and it's still not getting done!

What, Lord? Get some volunteers from the congregation to help? Yeah, sure. Make some phone calls. You too, Lord?! Thanks! Any time. Bye!

2

BURNOUT AND CODEPENDENCE

Given how often we hear and see it used, *burnout* may seem to be one of the most over- or misused words in the English vocabulary. Yet its seeming ubiquity may reflect its growing prevalence in American society. Relative to this book's intended usage, *Merriam-Webster* defines *burnout* as "exhaustion of physical or emotional strength or motivation usually as a result of prolonged stress or frustration."[1] Even those who may not be able to define the word in such formal terms likely can understand or relate to that description. Virtually everyone has experienced burnout relative to something in their life at one time or another. It doesn't take a professional to recognize that the clergyperson depicted in the previous chapter was well on the road toward burnout. Yet despite this book's title, burnout is in no way limited to the clergy; it is far more widespread.

But *Merriam-Webster* also defines *burnout* as "a person showing the effects of drug abuse,"[2] and this points to one of the primary ideas I want to raise about the nature of burnout. That is, *burnout* is too often a politically correct or "safe" term for a real disease—codependence. This is not to suggest a one-to-one equation of the two terms or to say that all burnout derives solely from codependence, but my years of working with pastors suggest to me that all too often, codependence plays a key role in the burnout issues of clergy. In short, burned-out clergy are as likely as not to exhibit codependent behaviors. For that reason, in this book, I will focus on codependence as a key factor in clergy burnout; while other factors may be at play as well—which have corresponding "responses"—I address what, in my experience, is the key precipitating factor.

DEFINING CODEPENDENCE

The term *codependence* originally comes from the field of addictions and their treatment. In the family system, codependence functions like this: One family member has an addiction, and in order for that person to remain in the family, all the other members of the family must be codependent. If the family fails to fulfill the codependent dynamics, then that person must either get sober or get out of the family. Like alcoholism or substance addiction, codependence is itself a "disease" that has become so common in our culture, we perceive it to be "normal" and therefore deny its relevance or its validity. Since we believe that such attitudes and behaviors are "normal," then why bother addressing them? Everybody does it. So what's the big deal? As Gerald May, MD, wrote in his classic *Addiction and Grace*, "I realized that for both myself and other people, addictions are not limited to substances."[3]

My own definition of codependence, which I amalgamate from many sources, reads, "A set of maladaptive behaviors that a person learns to survive in an experience of great emotional pain and stress and that are passed on from generation to generation. These behaviors and their accompanying attitudes are self-defeating and result in a diminished capacity. Codependents do not take adequate care of themselves and are far too controlled by (or controlling of) other peoples' behaviors and attitudes."

May lists a great number of what he calls "attraction addictions."[4] Some are obvious and even fun—candy, chocolate, coffee, ice cream, pistachio nuts, and pizza. But May also lists subtler addictions to such things as receiving approval; being good, helpful, loved, nice, and right; demonstrating competence; representing images of God; achieving performance; gaining popularity; having rewarding relationships; exercising responsibility; working hard; and proving worthiness. Obviously, this last grouping relates highly to the clergy.

In her book *Co-dependence: Misunderstood—Mistreated*, Anne Wilson Schaef claims that 80 percent of helping professionals suffer from codependence.[5] If this number is anywhere near accurate, it's little wonder that denial is so prevalent—at those levels, codependence appears to be "normal." Denial is one of the key symptoms of codependence; in fact, it cannot even exist without denial, which is one of the factors that makes this whole enterprise so daunting. How can we clergy own our part in this disease? How can we make the breakthrough?

Jesus says, "You will know the truth, and the truth will make you free" (John 8:32). Although he was not referring to codependence in those words, those who have worked with addicts have long known that knowing the truth is essential to people's finding freedom from their addictions. Indeed, if we have the courage to embrace the truth, we can be free. If we can gain support from our peers, we can be free. If we can get our congregations to acknowledge the truth, we can be free. If judicatory executives and denominational executives can have the fortitude to admit the truth, we can be free. This freedom is truly God's desire. Let us prayerfully and bravely seek that truth for ourselves and for the church. It will be a struggle, but a worthy struggle—for our lives, for our congregations, and for our souls.

RULES AND ROLES OF CODEPENDENCE

In order to sustain a disease as prolific as codependence, there must be something that gets "under the skin," that penetrates one's passions and takes control. There must be a force so powerful that we succumb to it far too easily. Nothing could reach that level of success without some order and direction. There must be rules to follow and roles to fulfill and certain characteristics to maintain. Codependence could not be as chaotic and haphazard as it is and still maintain such a powerful hold on people without these factors.

Studies of codependence in family systems suggest that dysfunctional families display traits that are distinctively different from healthy families. A comparative list appears in chapter 2. Many of those dysfunctional characteristics are easily recognizable in our congregations, and far too little evidence of the healthy characteristics exists in congregational ministry and ministers. Is it any wonder, then, that so many clergy reflect a diseased model of ministry?

Another familiar resource on codependence lists the behaviors that must be present in a family system to sustain an addiction. No one member manifests all the behaviors; the range of behaviors is commonly shared among the family. Reading through these behaviors, take note of how many are endemic to congregational life today, though they are rarely addressed:

Codependent Behaviors

- anger
- boundary violations or confusion
- caretaking
- control
- denial
- dependency
- difficulty having fun
- inappropriate intimacy
- inappropriate sexuality
- indirect communication
- low self-worth
- loyalty
- mistrust
- obsession
- sharing

It is also helpful to differentiate dysfunctional from healthy behaviors:

Dysfunctional	Healthy
Rigid, binary	*Open to change* and new ideas
Low self-worth, shame	*High self-worth*
Compulsive behavior covers pain	*People choose* their behavior
Rules are arbitrary, rigid, or nonexistent, chaos	*Rules are* designed to *guide*, and *protect*; age appropriate and consistent
Feelings are avoided and repressed; no risks taken, no safety	*Feelings are expressed* openly and validated; touch is appropriate and nurturing
Denial of stress, issues, and problems; stress is a welcomed distraction from emotional pain	*Expect stress*, pull together for mutual support
Disturbed hierarchy: one person or *no one* is in charge, hidden coalitions provide limited safety, may be upside down (children protecting parents) or chaos	*Parents are in charge*: strong coalition, they protect and assume responsibility for children
Terminal seriousness: anger, depression, hostility, or phony happiness	*Fun, humor, joy, and laughter* exist in adults and children

Related to these behaviors is a set of codependent roles. Again, no single member of a dysfunctional and codependent family system manifests all these roles; they are shared. Yet it is clear that these roles coincide with the expectations assigned to the parish clergy in our contemporary culture. We will review these roles one by one:

Chief enabler. In a dysfunctional family, one member must be the person who keeps things functioning. The family depends on this person, child or adult, to see that food is on the table and all is in order. In the congregation, that role falls to the clergy.

The "buck stops" with the clergy. Everyone expects the clergy to keep things in good order: to ensure that the worship services will happen and be done well, to oversee all the committees and organizations within the congregation, to be aware of the finances, to manage the staff, to run the building, and more. No one else in the congregation bears the same burden of enabling.

Scapegoat. In this light of their being chief enablers, when anything goes wrong, despite who actually did it, the clergy are held responsible. When failure belongs to the clergy rather than the members of the congregation, volunteers can function more easily. Since they will ultimately remain blameless, they are then free to serve at their own pleasure and convenience. The clergy will fill in the gaps and catch and correct all the mistakes in the nick of time so that no harm will be done. And if any harm does occur, the blame goes to the clergy.

Family hero. Someone in the family has to carry the "family honor." Who is the "good one" to whom everyone else can point with pride? Who is the one who will cast a sufficient shadow of righteousness so that all the others can live comfortably in its shade? Who will live up to the highest moral standards and thus liberate the others from such an ethical burden? Clearly, in a congregation, it is the clergy. No one else has to be as pure and faithful as the clergy. With the clergy in place to set an example for everyone else, the congregation can rest in the shadow of righteousness the pastors cast.

Lost child. In a dysfunctional family, one or more of the children is invisible, lost to the attention of all the others. Sometimes this is a desirable position to be in, since to be noticed is to be abused. Better to just be unseen, ignored, forgotten, hidden. Too often, in the congregation, it is the clergy who are in this role. While people know their clergyperson as just that, "clergy," who knows this human being in all their humanity? Who genuinely knows the clergy's fears and worries? Who knows their deep anxieties? Who bothers to ask in a sincere way how the pastor is doing? After all, the members are not there to care for the clergy; the clergy is there to care for the members. If the members see their clergyperson as weak and vulnerable, they feel insecure. If the clergyperson is their "enabler" and their "hero," how can they be less than superhuman? And if they are less than expected, the whole system begins to implode. This cannot be. There is no room for the clergyperson to be a mere mortal; after all, this is God's emissary. This person cannot be as frail and fragile as the members. That is not allowed. So the words of the old spiritual "Sometimes I feel like a motherless child" very often fit the clergy.

Rescuer. Not only is all responsibility placed on the clergy; so also is the expectation that no matter what calamity befalls the congregation or any of its members, the clergy will rush in and save the day. When mistakes are made, who turns everything right again? When suffering befalls a member, who is there to comfort and console? When there is sickness, who will pray for healing? When a problem arises, who will dictate the solution? *The clergy*—that's who! The clergy is in tune with God and can rescue, heal, turn sadness into joy and sorrow into comfort. The clergy will make all things right again.

Mascot. Addictive families must have some comic relief. Someone has to be the clown or the cheerleader who will break the tension of stress and despair. In the congregation, it is the clergy who serve as cheerleaders and sources of comic relief. It is the clergy to whom people turn for a word or an action that will break the tension and bring everything back to a comfortable level again. I know one clergyperson who was serving a congregation named Good Shepherd. The members all got T-shirts with their names on the back. For this clergyperson, in the place of the name, they put "Sheep Dog." How's that for a mascot?

MORE CHARACTERISTICS OF CODEPENDENCE

In addition to the characteristics of codependence listed previously, five specific symptoms of the disease deserve our attention here. One of these symptoms is *triangulation*. This is when two people, person A and person B, have an issue dividing them, and they go to person C to solve the problem. This thereby shifts the burden of finding a solution from persons A and B onto person C. This is routine behavior in the church. Parishioners will not deal directly with each other or with the congregational staff. Instead, they will seek to reel in the clergyperson in order to take the problem and its anxieties off their own shoulders.

In one of the congregations I served, I was confronted with a problem regarding the sexton. Several people had developed problems with him over how he arranged furniture in some rooms and other issues regarding the building, which grew into a significant conflict over power and territory. They came to me and insisted that I fix the problem, out of a belief that solving their problems was part of my job description as the resident clergy. By attempting to take the problem off their shoulders and put it on mine, they engaged in triangulation.

Rather than get drawn into that trap, I asked permission to use their names as I approached the sexton. Then I informed the sexton that *he* had a problem with these other people and that I expected *him* to talk directly with them and resolve it. I refused to take responsibility for the resolution. Instead, I empowered the sexton to address the problem directly and work it out.

Another characteristic of codependence is called *skilled incompetence*. This is when people use certain skills to disguise where they lack abilities or knowledge. For instance, some members of the congregation will misquote the denominational discipline to make their point or memorize select Bible verses to support their positions while ignoring other passages that contradict their agenda.

Externalization is another element inherent in codependence. In many instances, parishioners exercise what some call *transference*: they place on the clergyperson pain and discomfort they are feeling themselves. Plagued with the anxiety of their own problems, they seek to externalize or transfer that problem off of themselves and onto a willing martyr/victim. Sound familiar?

Being skilled in pastoral counseling, I often knew what was going on in the lives of my parishioners on a deeper level. I commonly would see them dumping frustration, fears, and anger onto innocent others—often on me, the pastor. Why? Because all the garbage that people carry regarding unfinished issues with parents and other authority figures finds a ready target in the clergy, who often play those same roles for church members. I will return to this theme of the pastor as parent later on.

As already noted, the church has raised *denial* to an art form. When I was a child, my aunt, who was also my Sunday school teacher, had a favorite expression: "Don't talk like that." That was her go-to phrase whenever the truth of the matter became exposed and the words were spoken out loud. "Don't talk like that" seems to be the motto of many churches: "We don't want to know the truth. We have our own 'truth' that has sustained our bigotry and prejudices for so long—don't confront or challenge us with *reality*. We prefer to live in denial. We prefer to remain intentionally ignorant. The change would be painful. It would mean admitting our faults and failures, our sins and disgrace." So rather than endure that pain, we just "won't talk like that."

Perhaps the most problematic symptom of codependence in the church is *perfectionism*. Many parishioners look upon the clergy, God's emissaries, as being holy themselves. And since they are so "pure and perfect," they will not disappoint the parishioners or say no to them. God would never let them down. God's emissaries ought to be the same—dedicated beyond reason, on duty 24/7, and always available for any and all requests.

And congregations have in their minds a model of the "perfect pastor." This model includes all those codependent roles: hero, martyr, enabler, and the rest. The perfect pastor bears the pains of the congregation on their behalf. The perfect pastor would never inflict pain upon a congregation, never cause anxiety or distress, and never act in a confrontational manner regarding difficult issues. Perfect pastors are here to make all the worries and woes go away!

One congregation I served had a serious problem with racism. For years I tried to deal with it in a collaborative manner, gentle and slow. But it eventually became evident that unless the racism was eliminated in a timely fashion, this congregation (mostly European Americans in

an African American community) would die. So rather than be a part-
ner in the demise, I began to shift from collaborative to confrontational approaches, naming the racism openly as the situation required.
The response I got was predictable: "How dare our pastor behave that
way? This is not appropriate behavior for a 'person of God!'" Or so
many of my members stated.

Be perfect, do everything right, don't make mistakes, never say a
word that might cause pain. Be the selfless martyr. Bear everyone else's
pains. Make everything right—that's the way to please God. Church
leaders will deny that this sort of works-righteousness is taught in congregations. But just ask the average church member what they believe.
It is pervasive among the laity. Bad things aren't supposed to happen
to good people. And when they do, the good people are thrown into
a dither: "How can this happen to me? I am a good church person!"

These five symptoms, coupled with the other characteristics and
roles already discussed, form the foundation for our coming to understand that our codependence preys upon certain personality types and
limits the options for clergypersons dealing with burnout. In the next
three chapters, we will look at those specific dimensions of the problem.

3

PERSONALITIES AND CODEPENDENCE

If Anne Wilson Schaef is correct in her claim that as many as 80 percent of those in the helping professions are codependent, then clearly, codependence is a pervasive reality that all in the congregational system need to address. Only with a solid understanding of the problem can we attempt to achieve a working solution. Simplistic answers will not suffice. The disease is deep and complicated, reinforced by many sources. Obtaining the desired wellness will require diligence, honesty, and strength. In particular, we will need to be informed, for only when we have sufficient information to assist us can we cut through denial on all of its many levels.

This extensive effort at diagnosis lays important groundwork for the business of recovery that can take place—not only personally but also for a system as large and steeped in tradition as the church. Having already reviewed the behaviors and roles that accompany codependence, we now move on to examine those personality types that are most susceptible to this disease. For the work here, I will employ insights from the Myers-Briggs Type Indicator (MBTI), the world's most widely used personality-type instrument. Many seminaries use it routinely with their students, as do many pastoral candidacy groups. It is likely most readers have had some exposure to it and that you know your own personality type. For those as yet unfamiliar, I invite you to compare yourself to the various options and discern your personality type and thus its part in shaping your own codependence.

UNDERSTANDING PERSONALITIES AND TEMPERAMENTS

The MBTI measures preferences along four scales: Extravert (E) or Introvert (I), Sensing (S) or Intuitive (N), Thinking (T) or Feeling (F), Judging (J) or Perceiving (P). In turn, these four scales render sixteen possible combinations, such as ENFP, INFP, ENTP, ISFJ, and so on. Research from the MBTI provides some approximate breakdowns of the US population according to gender along each of the four scales as well as some comparative statistics regarding clergy. The Thinking–Feeling scale, which measures on what basis one prefers to make decisions, holds some particular insights for our purposes here. *Thinkers* are characteristically nonpersonal, objective, analytical, questioning, always seeking clarity, and linear in their approach. They are rational, logical in their processing, and not swayed by emotions. *Feelers*, on the other hand, are characteristically very emotional, personal, subjective, sentimental, agreeing, harmonizing, and circular in their approach. Thinkers make decisions with their heads; feelers make decisions with their hearts. Thinkers enjoy debate and the energy of a discussion no matter how heated; feelers detest conflict of any kind and will go to extremes to avoid it, even to being overly appeasing.

Examining the statistics related to the Thinking–Feeling scale, one notes an almost equal breakdown in the overall population between the two poles. Broken down by gender, however, 65 percent of US males show a preference for Thinking as opposed to 35 percent who prefer Feeling, while US females show the exact opposite preference: 65 percent Feeling versus 35 percent Thinking. Remarkably, however, among clergy of both genders, the numbers are as follows: Thinking = 32 percent; Feeling = 68 percent.

Now obviously, this does not take into account the strength of one's preference. The stronger the preference, the more profound the characteristics will be. Nevertheless, this makes it obvious that we need to start focusing our efforts on the Feelers.

When the characteristics of codependence are compared to those of the Feeling preference, we see obvious similarities. Codependent behaviors like caretaking, being loyal, and sharing are endemic to

Feelers. Codependent roles like enabling, rescuing, and being a mascot are likewise second nature for Feelers. Since they hate conflict, the mascot role of comic relief and cheerleader is quite comfortable.

This, of course, does not discount the insights that can be gleaned from a further examination of the sixteen MBTI types; for our purposes in this book, however, a full understanding of all the different personality types is not necessary. For such information, I recommend the book *Please Understand Me* by David Keirsey and Marilyn Bates.[1] In addition, *Personality Types and Religious Leadership* by Roy Oswald and Otto Kroeger does a good job of relating the MBTI to pastoral ministry.[2] What is helpful to know here is that Keirsey and Bates discovered that it is appropriate to reduce the sixteen types to four pairs known as *temperaments*: Intuitive–Feeling (NF), Intuitive–Thinking (NT), Sensing–Judging (SJ), and Sensing–Perceiving (SP). Three of these four temperaments, which I will examine here briefly, have special relevance as they relate to the tendency toward codependence among clergy. To help readers remember these three temperaments, I have given each a name that serves as shorthand for a significant characteristic of that temperament.

The NF Temperament: Guilty Gus

Those with the NF temperament—Intuitive–Feeling—might be called the "Guilty Guses" of the world. While NFs make up only 12 percent of the general population, this is the most common temperament among clergy, according to Oswald and Kroeger, representing 40 to 48 percent of male clergy and over 51 percent of female clergy. For this reason, we will pay particular attention to them in this chapter.

Putting the Intuitive personality preference with the Feeling preference only serves to magnify the Feeling characteristics. Intuitives are otherworldly, dreamy, visionary, abstract, theoretical, imaginative, and symbol oriented. They are highly idealistic and not down-to-earth. Combining such idealism with the people orientation of the Feeling preference makes NFs all the more prone to codependence. Guilty Guses hate conflict even more than Feelers in any other combination.

They are more sensitive and moved by emotions. Codependent roles like chief enabler, family hero, rescuer, and even lost child are naturals. They will give to a fault and dedicate themselves to the care of others, not thinking of their own well-being. Most important (and obvious), Guilty Guses do guilt! They feel the pain of guilt far too easily and are thus more likely manipulated, controlled, and used than are others. The idealism of a Guilty Gus sparks him or her to heights of sacrifice and noble action. They are the Don Quixotes of the world—show them a windmill, and they fly into action.

Most disturbing is that codependent NFs are more likely than any other temperament to demonstrate poor boundary maintenance; that is, they cross other people's boundaries inappropriately and allow others to cross their boundaries inappropriately. At the Church Renewal Center, most of our cases involved inappropriate boundary crossing, particularly clergy sexual impropriety, such as having an affair with a parishioner. Almost universally, these clients were Fs—most of them NFs—whose need for personal interaction, sentimentality, and emotional satisfaction and their being a "lost child" made that clergyperson vulnerable to poor boundary maintenance and acting out sexually.

The SJ Temperament: By the Book

Sensing–Judging (SJ) is the second most frequent temperament for clergy—call them the "By the Books." Oswald and Kroeger note that 36 percent of male clergy (but only 7 percent of female clergy) are SJ. Those with the Sensing preference are more grounded in the here and now than are Intuitives and are very down-to-earth, while Judgers seek resolution and completion and are bottom-line people. When put together, however, they are highly duty bound, driven to "get it right." They are strictly by-the-book people who love tradition and resist change vehemently. Stability and maintenance of the status quo are their primary aims; thus they are controlled by what has gone before. If the "normal" way of doing things that is affirmed and rewarded by the system is codependent, then By the Books are going to be codependent or die! They will not question the tradition but will be totally faithful to it: "That's the way it's always been, and that's the way it should always be." Change is the enemy even if change means health and improvement. The tried and true, so it seems, rules the day. Therefore, a codependent system like the church will foster and nurture By the Book codependents, who will be masters at denial and fierce defenders of the tradition. Don't rock the boat; keep the steady course even if it leads to destruction.

The NT Temperament: Gotta Be Right

The other temperament I want to explore from a codependent perspective is the Intuitive–Thinker (NT), who could be called "Gotta Be Right." Oswald and Kroeger estimate that 16 percent of male clergy and 25 percent of the female clergy are NTs. As noted earlier, Intuitives are idealistic dreamers, while Thinkers are normally rational and linear. But the combination of that idealism and rationality turns NTs into perfectionists. They are always trying to do "it" better. They are not satisfied until everything is excellent. The threat that they might be seen as incompetent is intolerable.

When inserted into a codependent system that defines excellence in codependent terms, even Gotta Be Rights are subject to the pressure to comply with the system's demands. Since they need to be recognized as having done "it" better than others, they will strive to reach new heights of enabling performance and become more of the family hero and rescuer than others. They have the best ways, and they are eager to demonstrate their superior skills. Unlike Guilty Guses, Gotta Be Rights will not approach the task from an emotional stance but will address the situation in a cognitive manner that is predetermined by the pressures of a codependent environment. They will perform in a codependent style to a higher level of achievement.

Adding It Up

If you add up Oswald and Kroeger's figures, NFs, SJs, and NTs compose nearly 100 percent of male clergy and 83 percent of female clergy.

Of course, not all of these clergy will suffer the ill effects of codependence, but the very fact that so many have personality preferences that show tendencies toward codependence makes clear that gaining their support for overthrowing this disease and remaking the culture in which it thrives will not be easy. Let's face it: idealistic people persons like the Guilty Guses and ardent protectors of tradition like the By the Books, who make up the vast majority of clergy, will *not* be the vanguard of a movement to change that culture.

Guilty Guses (NFs) are not as resistant to change as are By the Books (SJs), but they strongly avoid conflict. To challenge an entire culture and remake values, norms, behaviors, attitudes, and even beliefs will be such a huge endeavor that Guilty Guses may not have the heart or stomach for it. They will not endure in the battle. They will feel their own and others' pain too deeply. The guilt of disrupting and disturbing others will be too much, and they will retreat.

The combination of NFs, SJs, and NTs totaling such a large percentage of the clergy is a daunting statistic to overcome. Is there any wonder why this disease has been so ingrained for generations? Is there any wonder why the denial is so intense? Is there any wonder why pleas to address this disease have fallen on deaf ears for so long? Unless clergy grow tired enough of being victimized and grow impatient with being rescuers and scapegoats to face the truth and be free, codependence will continue to work its destructive power upon the church. Like any addiction, it is an enormous battle to become free. But it can happen. And for the sake of the church and its people, it must happen.

TEMPERAMENT CHARACTERISTICS AND BOUNDARIES

When one examines more closely some of the characteristics of these temperaments, it is easy to understand why these three dispositions are most prone to codependence. For instance, as noted previously, Guilty Guses (NFs) are particularly prone to inappropriate boundary crossing. Anne Wilson Schaef, in *Co-dependence: Misunderstood—Mistreated*, talks about "relationship addiction," stating, "Codependents are relationship addicts who frequently use a relationship in the same way drunks use alcohol: to get a 'fix.'"[3] Such a strong dependence leads to poor boundary definition: "Codependents literally do not know where they end and others begin."[4] Since they have no boundaries, codependents take on others' sadness, happiness, fear, or whatever people around them are feeling or thinking. They tend to personalize everything that happens around them and see it as directly related to themselves. This symptom/characteristic is called *enmeshment*. Guilty Guses frequently get enmeshed with their parishioners out of their deep desire to help. Their "relationship addiction" becomes evident in a need-to-be-needed attitude.

Second, Guilty Guses are so emotionally intense, they cannot comprehend or experience *indifference*. They are so people oriented that the very idea of not getting personally involved is almost immoral. How can we treat other people as objects, with indifference? That seems sinful. For NFs, what the world needs is more person-to-person sensitivity, more compassion, more tenderheartedness, and more daring to listen and respond to one another's concerns. Indifference seems cold and aloof.

In the same way, Guilty Guses cannot comprehend that others might be indifferent toward them. Since indifference is not in their realm of experience or seems almost evil, then understanding that others might be indifferent toward them is totally foreign. When someone is indifferent, Guilty Guses perceive it as dislike, when the truth is that the other is merely uninterested.

Lacking the option of indifference makes normal boundary maintenance that much more difficult. Everything becomes like or dislike. And since being disliked is painful for a Guilty Gus, they will go to extremes to be liked—or even better, to be loved. To achieve that purpose, they must also manage people's impressions. If it is necessary to be liked by everyone, then codependents must be able to control other peoples' attitudes toward them.

This leads, finally, to the inability to say no. In their endless quest for that interpersonal affirmation, saying no is counterproductive. Guilty Guses find it nearly impossible to turn down the request of a parishioner. Since Guilty Guses raise the experience of guilt to a near art form, the very last thing they can hear is a parishioner saying, "You weren't there when I needed you." Guilty Guses would rather be tortured than fail to meet the needs of others. They cannot disappoint others, they cannot hurt others, they cannot let others down. Guilt is such a powerful force for them that they would rather deny themselves and sacrifice their own needs than "not be there" for others.

A personal illustration: In one of my early parishes, I had forty shut-ins living in four different counties. In order to give at-home communions to all of them, I would leave early in the morning and be gone all day. I'd stop by the house for a quick supper and then head out again for a church meeting. On one such day, my son (then four years old) said, "So long, Dad. Thanks for stopping by." Ouch! I was caught. How could I ignore my shut-ins? And how could I ignore my family? "Thanks for stopping by . . ." It was a painful dilemma. I chose my family.

In the same way, both Guilty Guses and Gotta Be Rights are compelled to please others, to solve other people's problems. Guilty Guses act out of compassion. Gotta Be Rights, on the other hand, act out of a sense of competence. As Schaef states, "Believing that you *should* have a solution is a characteristic of codependence. Codependents want to please. When they cannot, they believe they are personal failures and try to hide the fact that they cannot meet everyone's expectations."[5] Pleasing is Guilty Gus; avoiding failure is Gotta Be Right. Caretaking is the result; being indispensable closely follows.

At the Church Renewal Center, one clergyperson told us about three elderly ladies in his congregation who all lived in the same house. Eventually, one of them could no longer go up the steps to her bedroom. She could come down the steps to the first floor, where she handled most of her daily functions, but walking back up was impossible for her. The solution was that the clergy would stop by the house and *carry* this dear lady up to her bedroom—every evening. Talk about being indispensable, caretaking, needing to be needed, and being an enabler, hero, rescuer, and all the rest!

Codependents are meddlers; they believe it is their moral duty to be involved. They can and should be able to fix anything—that is what

God demands of a pastor. So much gets intertwined in their lives. In so many ways and at so many levels, they are so personally enmeshed with the lives of others and the congregation that they no longer know where they begin and where they end. In order to sustain this enmeshed status, clergy need to deny their own feelings. How can we clergy admit how taxing and impossible our pastoral roles have become and still be the heroes and enablers that our people desire us to be? How can we bear the pain and confusion that must result from such boundary diffusion and continue on in the role? How can we totally deny ourselves and live the selfless life we have been taught?

Easy: only "acceptable" feelings can be felt. Clergy must learn to adapt their feelings to the pressures of the congregation. Yet such a distortion of feelings can create resentment, anger, and even depression due to the growing dishonesty with oneself. Moreover, when feelings, perceptions, and boundaries become so confused, codependents are vulnerable to believe anything they are told, particularly Guilty Guses. So concerned with pleasing others, with being accepted, and with being compassionate, they easily become gullible. Guilty Guses would rather swallow a fabrication than risk hurting someone's feelings. The possibility of alienating and not supporting another is unthinkable—tantamount to evil.

By the Books (SJs), while not singled out as much in this chapter, fall prey to many of the same issues because they are so dedicated to maintaining the status quo. And when the status quo is so infused with codependence, the By the Books are obligated to comply. Regardless of what temperament best describes you or the clergyperson you know best, I hope that by now, we all are getting a clearer and more complete picture of the disease of codependence and its many characteristics, symptoms, and outcomes. The next chapter will put all this into a graphic that I believe is very helpful.

4

THE CHURCH AND CODEPENDENCE

When clergy tell stories of discontent and frustration, yearn for the day they can retire, and report that practicing the work of God has lowered their self-esteem, then something is dramatically wrong. Nevertheless, we've made some significant progress on our journey to understand and begin to recover from our addiction to codependence. Every step, every tool that brings greater clarity moves us closer to the health and freedom we so desire. Understanding the congregations in which this codependence is nurtured is a key factor in gaining such clarity.

Those who study congregations often focus their work based on the size of the gathering and the qualities that characterize like-size groups. Likely a majority of American congregations fall into what is called the "pastor-centered" size category—those churches with an average worship attendance of 50 to 150. This designation may be an indication of just how institutionalized this sort of codependence has become. The "pastor-centered" church has its own characteristics: everything centers on the pastor, the pastor relates to everyone, expectations are high for the pastor to manage and control everything, growth depends on the popularity of the pastor, communication centers on the pastor, the pastor recruits and shepherds new members and volunteers, and the pastor is on an intimate level with all members even at the expense of attention to the pastor's spouse and family. This is addictive fodder for the Guilty Guses, the Gotta Be Rights, and even the By the Books.

THE CODEPENDENCY GRAPH

Clearly, when you match up the overwhelming number of pastors who have temperaments that are prone to codependent behaviors with the thousands of "pastor-centered" congregations that dot the US landscape, you have the makings of a seriously dysfunctional church scene in dire need of diagnosis and healing. Donald Hands, former clinical director of the St. Barnabas Center in Wisconsin (a program similar to the Church Renewal Center where I served), developed an important tool in this diagnostic process: the codependency graph (see chapter 4).[1] Dr. Hands put together this graph based on his experience and clinical knowledge working with church professionals; I have reworked the graph to make it more user-friendly.

Now, grab ahold of your courage and dare to walk with me through all the aspects of this graph. We have embraced a lot so far, but this tool may well be the one that penetrates our denial and opens to us the truth more than anything else. This graph provides the best overview of the pathology in the church that I have found. It makes the reality so clear that it becomes hard to ignore and even harder to deny.

As you can see, the graph is created by two axes. The horizontal axis measures *satisfaction and success in ministry*: the right end of the axis indicates maximum satisfaction in relationships with parishioners and a rewarding and successful ministry; the left end indicates poor or painful relationships with parishioners and a conflicted, failing, or even neglected ministry. The vertical axis measures *personal care*: the top end of the axis indicates maximum self-esteem, self-care, and a healthy, solid personal identity; the bottom end points to low self-esteem, lack of a healthy and solid personal identity, and poor or neglected personal care. Overlapping the two axes produces four quadrants that designate (starting from the upper right and moving counterclockwise) (I) interdependence, (II) hidden codependence, (III) hopelessness, and (IV) codependency. We will look at each in turn.

Codependency graph

	Maximum Self-esteem, self-care, personal identity		
Minimum Relationships with others Negative/conflicted, painful/neglected, failure	**II. Hidden codependency** Dominance, control, grandiosity Enmeshment phobia, "hero" role and mentality "I matter, you don't matter" (small percentage)	**I. Interdependence** Honesty closeness / healthy boundaries "I matter, you matter" (very rare)	**Maximum** Relationships with others Positive, rewarding, successful
	III. Hopelessness Despair, depression, isolation Active addictions: substances, food, work, sex, religion Suicide potential (physical, emotional, spiritual) Numbed feelings, "lost child" role and mentality "Nothing matters, nothing ever really changes" (fastest growing)	**IV. Codependency** Submission martyr / victim abandonment phobia Enmeshment "You matter, I don't matter" (normative)	
	Minimum No or low self-esteem, no personal identity, personal neglect / lack of self-care		

Quadrant I: Interdependence

Quadrant I is called the "interdependence" quadrant for the positive and healthy interaction that takes place. Key characteristics of this quadrant are full and complete honesty (especially regarding one's feelings) and closeness to others while maintaining healthy boundaries. This is the "I matter, you matter" quadrant. Here ministry is satisfying and successful, and there is good self-care.

I have labeled this quadrant as "very rare," as I have yet to see for myself any congregation that genuinely and fully fits here, despite my longtime exposure to numerous congregations in a wide variety of denominations throughout the nation. When clergy tell me that they are serving in such a congregation, I ask them how long they have been there, and they almost always reply, "Less than a year." In other words, they are still in the "honeymoon stage" of ministry in that congregation. I ask them to get back to me in five years if they still believe they are in a quadrant I congregation. I have yet to have a single one reiterate their claim.

How does one assess whether one is in a quadrant I congregation? The quick-and-dirty (as opposed to scientific and refined) test has to do with feelings and honesty. Imagine a continuum where positive feelings like joy, happiness, hope, and love represent one pole, and negative feelings like frustration, disappointment, and anger represent the other end. Clergy are generally permitted to express all the feelings we want from the positive end of the continuum, but expressing feelings on the negative end is not allowed.

Let me illustrate with a personal example: One congregation I served for a number of years, although it was thriving, did not offer me a pay raise for three years despite dramatic cost-of-living increases at that time. The excuse for no raise was that the escalating cost of health insurance (which they paid) exceeded whatever raise I might have expected. My children were in elementary school at the time and were eager to pursue such activities as dance lessons, musical lessons, gymnastics, and so forth. But with my stagnant wages, we found ourselves having to say to our children more and more often, "We can't afford . . ."

Finally, I went to the congregation's governing board and told them, "Watching the lifestyle of my family deteriorate as I continue on as your pastor is causing me a morale problem." I made no threats or ultimatums; I simply shared my feelings of concern and discomfort. Shortly after making that statement, I accepted a call to a new ministry. Prior to my departure from the congregation, one of the members of the church board approached me and reminded me of the statement I had made. He said, "Up until that point, I thought you were one of the finest parish pastors I had ever met. But from that point on, you were not fit for ministry." In one brief statement, I went from the top of the heap to unfit for duty! So much for honesty in parish ministry.

Without the opportunity for honesty about the whole range of feelings surrounding pastoral ministry, interdependence is practically not an option in the parish. While judicatory staff and other church leaders widely acknowledge this, they are doing little to address the phenomenon. That leaves clergy only quadrants II, III, and IV as places where they can dwell.

Quadrant II: Hidden Codependence

In quadrant II, clergy are struggling to maintain some kind of self-care in the face of unsatisfactory or failing ministry. Donald Hands calls this the "hidden codependency" quadrant; its key characteristics are dominance, control, grandiosity, and what Hands calls "enmeshment phobia." Clergy in this quadrant feel they know all the answers and are superior to the laity, and they therefore demand that the laity follow their leadership. As a result, clergy begin to fear that if they get too close to the laity, they might become enmeshed in the laity's mediocrity and thus be contaminated or lose their superior status. The clergy's attitude is that they are the "hero/heroine" called to rescue the laity from disbelief (or meager belief) and mediocrity and raise them to higher standards.

One clergyperson told me that his parishioners were, in his words, "spiritual pygmies"—meaning they were weak and shallow in their faith—and that it was his goal for his ministry to make them all "spiritual giants." In other words, the magnificence of his ministry would raise them to new heights of faith and courage. How grandiose and superior—and what dominance and control must be exercised for such an enterprise! Hands calls this a "hidden codependence," since it is a less obvious role for some than the martyr/victim role.

Clergy in quadrant II will be tempted to micromanage everything and sometimes everybody. The issue is control, one of the key characteristics of codependence. This is especially tempting for SJs, who are basically into control anyway, and for NTs, who are into competency and will use control to achieve results that meet their demanding standards.

Clergy who micromanage programs and events are bad enough, but those who attempt to micromanage other people's lives are even worse: "Look, this is what you ought to do. And if you won't do that, then stop bothering me. Why do you ask for my help if you won't do what I tell you to do?" Clergy who need to have dominance and control will believe that they know best and have the "divine duty" to rescue the misguided members from all their mistakes. While this may appear to be benevolent, it is an insidious behavior that in the long run strips people of the freedom to run their own lives and builds an unhealthy, counterproductive dependence on the clergy. Driven by this need to be the "grand master" of the congregation, quadrant II clergy become enmeshed, attached, and overwhelmed—only they cannot admit it because that would be a disallowed sign of weakness. Constrained by their passion to be at the top of it all, they will put themselves in impossible situations and then blame everyone else for causing them such hardship. If only the members of the congregation weren't so inept, then a quadrant II clergy would not have to become so overburdened.

I have labeled this quadrant as a "small percentage," since I believe that very few congregations tolerate such attitudes and behaviors from their clergy. Some may believe that this is the kind of clergy they need to develop a strong and successful ministry—until they get one! Then the complaints soon fly to the judicatory executive in great numbers and the ministry is terminated (or the clergy self-destruct, as did the clergy who thought his people were "spiritual pygmies").

Quadrant III: Hopelessness

Quadrant III, which represents the combination of poor self-esteem and lack of self-care along with dissatisfaction with or failure in ministry, is the fastest growing of the four quadrants. According to Hands, here we see despair, depression, isolation, and possible addictions, such as to substances, food, and sex. I would also cite addictions to work and the misuse of religion.

Those in quadrant III have an increased chance of suicide—and not simply a physical suicide but an emotional or spiritual suicide. Feelings go numb; one's public affect becomes flat. Since one is not allowed to have negative feelings, it is easier to turn off those feelings and go numb. Internally and subconsciously, however, the feelings rage on. One has a sense of being a "lost child"—that no one really cares and that one's feelings, wants, and desires are ignored. The clergyperson believes that they have been abandoned at a very deep level to the point where nothing matters anymore.

Thus it is obvious why quadrant III is called the "hopelessness" quadrant. Clergy report to me increasingly that, after trying all the latest and greatest materials for church growth, stewardship, religious education, and all the rest, when all is said and done, nothing has really changed. So why bother? Nothing *ever* really changes. Despite the fact that this quadrant is the fastest growing, in my experience, judicatory and denominational leaders do not have an adequate handle on it. Most likely this is because they are often a part of the disease themselves and thus not sufficiently aware of its presence in their systems and its negative consequences to take appropriate action. Thus we pay far less attention to it than we should.

Quadrant IV: Codependency

In quadrant IV, we find the ministry to be satisfying and successful but at the expense of self-esteem and self-care. This is the way most people want their congregations to operate: the clergy are to be submissive and serve the people; the people should not serve the clergy. Clergy are the resident martyrs and victims on behalf of the congregation. The clergy can be taken for granted, overworked, underpaid, and even abused, and that is to be tolerated. Clergy are not allowed to complain; complaining shows a weakness in one's dedication. Clergy are compliant with this because of what Hands calls "abandonment phobia": "God forbid, they might reject me." Clergy, especially Guilty Guses, will go to extremes to be accepted into the fellowship and seek to gain the benefits of warm relationships with the members—the pats on the back they so desperately need.

On the other hand, since this is the normal set of expectations and the standard for competency, Gotta Be Rights are constrained to comply for fear of looking incompetent: "Why aren't you working seventy or eighty hours a week like most clergy? What's the matter with you? Are you inferior? Are you not dedicated? You're not measuring up to the standards." In a similar way, since this is "the tradition" set for clergy, By the Books are eager to sustain this style and accept it as the way things always have been and always should be.

Living as the resident martyr and victim, one soon becomes enmeshed in the pathology of the system. Boundaries get blurred. Personal identity evaporates. Clergy have told me that outside of their ministries, they have no idea who they are. Without their role, they are nobody. Somewhere in the first five years of their ministry, they lost track of themselves and learned that this was the price to survive in a classic codependent system.

Hands once referred to this as the "you matter, I don't matter" quadrant. It is normative in parish ministry because *it works*—as long as the clergy are willing to make the sacrifices. And of course, not only the clergyperson but also the clergy spouse and family must sacrifice for the sake of the system.

Many clergy spouses have shared with me their resentment of the church for taking away their partners. Yet they believe they dare not protest, since their spouse is doing "God's work"—it would seem sinful and cause them guilt to ask their spouse to take time away from something so important to attend to family matters. As Anne Wilson Schaef and Diane Fassel write in *The Addictive Organization*,

"When loyalty to the organization becomes a substitute for living one's own life, then the company has become the addictive substance of choice."[2]

What congregation brags about how wonderful their clergyperson is because she never fails to take at least two days off every week like most people do? What congregation brags that their clergyperson always uses all his vacation and continuing education time? How many laypeople think that is just wonderful and the sign of an effective ministry? What congregation offers a membership to the local gym as a standard perk to encourage their pastor to practice good exercise patterns? *None that I know.*

Clergy who are dependent on pats on the back in ministry will be on duty 24/7. They will go to extremes to keep everyone happy and never stir up any controversy, however appropriate that controversy may be. They will sacrifice time for themselves and their family and do so without one single complaint. That's the way the system is structured these days. That's the norm. And that's the norm that judicatory and denominational staff model as well. It is a disease infused throughout the system. Good health and proper boundaries are rare. Schaef and Fassel state it well: "The good martyr is the typical codependent who works selflessly for others and never attends to his or her own needs. We have heard of 'designer drugs'; *workaholism* may be the designer drug for the church."[3]

It's the workaholic who gets rewarded in the church. In his book *The Parboiled Pastor,* Lutheran pastor Steven McKinley writes, "The deepest fear we all have as pastors [is] the fear that we are being judged by our people and that someplace, somewhere, sometime someone will find us wanting, which will then lead us to judge ourselves as wanting. That keeps us pastors knocking ourselves out to do the very best job we can in everything we do. Such fear is a constant companion for many a parish pastor."[4]

McKinley continues with a classic codependent statement: "In truth, while we never hope for emergencies, they do *bring a measure of ego gratification* with them. There is a certain sense of satisfaction and fulfillment. What's more, *having people dependent on you makes you feel important*. You sure do show up the rest of those pastors whose people *don't need them nearly as much as your people need you*."[5] Is it important that we have this feeling, or does it justify our existence? For me, this is a smoking gun of codependency.

I've played the martyr/victim role myself: One of the congregations I served was hit by an arsonist who went through the valley burning churches and elementary schools. At about 4:00 a.m. one Sunday, I was notified that our church building was on fire. I immediately drove to the church and for hours, I crawled in and out of that building on my hands and knees to rescue the archives that went back over two hundred years, even though I nearly collapsed several times from the smoke. I just could not let them go up in flames, nor the communion ware, which I rescued next. I repeatedly risked my life and was exhausted.

That evening, we gathered in the local Methodist church to pull ourselves together and express thanks to God that no one was hurt. Congregants made speech after speech thanking the many firefighters who came from near and far to fight the flames. However, not one word was said about their pastor, who had risked his life for the congregation. I was their servant—such behavior was merely expected. And I was more than willing to sacrifice myself to hear the words of thanks, which never came.

MOVING FROM CODEPENDENCE TO INTERDEPENDENCE

It is important to note that the journey from quadrant IV to quadrant I has very little to do with our relationship with our parishioners and everything to do with our relationship with ourselves. The movement is on the axis of self-care, plain and simple. It is fully about how we treat ourselves as well as our spouses and families.

To make the move from quadrant IV to quadrant I is to swim upstream, against the current. It is countercultural. It will not get one pats on the back but, instead, will evoke questions of one's dedication and even faith. Congregations that are caught in the cycle of codependency will attempt to punish clergy who try to make this move by various methods of showing their displeasure, such as minimal or no pay raises. Codependent congregations will not rush to your side and defend your noble cause. That is not to say that you won't find individuals within the congregation who will be enlightened enough to encourage your pilgrimage to health and well-being. But more often than not, the organization as a whole will not support this move; you will need to fight for what you want. The system wants clergy to be in quadrant IV and will use all its influence to put them there and keep them there. That's where the rewards are. That's what keeps the parishioners happiest.

And we need to understand that ministry is not the only profession that demands such a sacrifice. Schaef and Fassel argue that this is now common in most professions. While it is especially rampant in the helping professions, business and industry are also guilty of these kinds of demands. The primary difference is that people in those professions are not seen as God's emissaries and therefore held to an even higher standard of dedication and sacrifice.

I am not talking about sacrificing ministry for the sake of saving oneself. It is possible to engage in productive ministry while maintaining healthy boundaries of self-care and family/spouse devotion. Obviously, staying in quadrant IV is an option, and that is what many so-called successful clergy do—they simply endure. They and their families pay the price. Is it any wonder, then, that clergy have an abnormally high incidence of mental illness, especially depression? That such a reality exists is a very sad commentary on the church.

For those seeking to escape this form of codependence, however, there are three choices. One may move to quadrants I (interdependence), II (hidden codependence), or III (hopelessness). Let's start with the movement to quadrant II.

Movement to Hidden Codependence

Anyone with even just one ounce of self-esteem will find it increasingly difficult to endure under the constant pressure to be submissive, to be the resident martyr/victim of quadrant IV. Eventually, however, one will begin to experience disappointment and disillusionment. The dream of a ministry that is interdependent with the parishioners and appropriately shares the joys and burdens of ministry slowly evaporates as the reality takes hold. It becomes clear that the burden is disproportionately on the clergy.

Consequently, disillusionment develops, which grows into disappointment. As the condition goes on, disappointment moves into frustration. From frustration arises resentment, and then sadness. From sadness, we ultimately arrive at anger with the congregation for "doing this to me," for "treating me like this"—never mind that we were fully complicit in the arrangement. We allowed it to happen to us. We played the game.

Often anger is not readily admitted, even to oneself. Therefore, we need a way to assess the indirect signs or expressions of anger. What follow are three lists of how anger may be manifest in an indirect way (keep in mind that these lists are not exhaustive; these are simply the most common manifestations):

Experiencing Anger through Physical Symptoms

1. Muscle tension
2. Headaches
3. Backaches
4. Stomach aches
5. Insomnia
6. Excessive sleeping
7. Loss of appetite
8. High blood pressure
9. Chronic fatigue
10. Constriction of the throat
11. Sexual difficulties
12. Trembling

Diverting Anger to Other Feelings

1. Depression
2. Guilt
3. Anxiety
4. Hostility
5. Resentment
6. Lethargy or boredom
7. Numbness or lack of feelings

Acting Anger Out in Indirect Ways

1. Hostile joking
2. Overreacting to situations
3. Physical violence
4. Physical activity
5. Constant activity
6. Daydreaming
7. Sulking
8. Frowning or scowling
9. Overeating
10. Careless driving
11. Accident proneness
12. Frequent forgetting
13. Crying
14. Abuse of alcohol or drugs
15. Abuse of prescription drugs
16. Constant criticizing
17. Spartan self-denial, such as severe dieting

Much of the process for developing this anger can be identified by what is called the codependent hate triangle, which involves a three-step process. *Step one*: We take care of other people's responsibilities for them; we enable them. *Step two*: We get mad at *them* for what *we've* done. *Step three*: We feel used and sorry for ourselves and act that out in anger or depression.

In our anger, we generally make one of two choices, neither one healthy. One is to move to quadrant II (hidden codependence) and adopt a superior attitude (the other option, moving to quadrant III, hopelessness, I discuss in what follows). We will take charge and not allow this nonsense to go on any longer. We will show them their wrongs, prove their inadequacies, and thus rescue them from their errors and mediocrity. We are the ones with the theological education. We have been trained in Scripture. We know how things are supposed to go. So it only makes sense that we rise up and grab authority. Domination is the way to get things done. Left up to the laity, it will never happen. And we're tired of being abused while we tolerate going nowhere.

My first call in ministry was as an assistant pastor in youth ministry, working under a hidden codependent pastor. His style was to *tell* the members what to do rather than engage with them in the work of the congregation. As a result, there was a constant feeling of tension as the members resisted being treated like "spiritual pygmies" and the pastor sought to control them. To no one's surprise, he suffered a major heart attack.

Such a movement to quadrant II happens with some frequency, but such efforts to dominate the congregation are ill-advised for many reasons. It is not the best way to do ministry, and it just doesn't work. After all, the laity outnumber the clergy. They are not fools—they know when their power is threatened or wrongly appropriated. They have had control for a long time and will not relinquish it without a fight. Sooner or later, they will either subdue or reject the clergyperson—or, as in the case of my first congregation, the dominating pastor may have a heart attack. None of those options are good. This is one reason why involuntary terminations of clergy have reached an all-time high in the United States.

Movement to Hopelessness

An alternative that is far more generally adopted is to take that growing frustration, resentment, sadness, and anger and move to quadrant III, the quadrant of hopelessness and depression.

One definition of depression is anger turned inward. Instead of beating up on the congregation (like with hidden codependence), we will beat up on ourselves. We tell ourselves that we must be the reason for the failure. While there is some element of truth to that, it doesn't take into account the enormous pressure exercised by the entire system. We are but one part of the total system that is enmeshed in this codependent process. To take *all* the blame upon oneself is inappropriate; to take no blame on oneself is characteristic of hidden codependence and is also inappropriate.

The correct approach is to place proper responsibility where it belongs. What was our part in the problem? Accept responsibility for that and for that alone. The system is too big for one person to carry all the burden. The codependence has become so ubiquitous that responsibility belongs at every corner of the organization and every level of the denomination.

Those who make the move to quadrant III give up hope. They become vulnerable to addiction to food and substances—anything to give a feeling of escape, ease the pain, and reduce the suffering, which we all know never works. Moreover, in the hopelessness quadrant, clergy become easy prey for sexual misconduct. I suspect that most pastors have had a member say something like, "Why didn't I find *you* to marry [instead of my terrible spouse]?" or "You understand me like no one else" or other similar comments. If we are emotionally and spiritually mired in hopelessness, then we are far more vulnerable to the temptations such comments offer. Why not? Nothing matters. Might as well . . .

Here's the typical scenario: When ministry fails to meet one's needs and one's self-esteem is falling, along comes an admirer who desires to show appreciation for some act of kindness we gave. Thus the stage is set for misconduct. It is a slippery slope that begins not with a full-fledged affair but rather with some small indiscretion that escapes the notice of others. Having "succeeded" with this little transgression, taking one small step after another to increasingly larger indiscretions is all too easy. It often happens without overt intention; it just happens. And by the time it becomes public, it is too late, and the individuals involved, their families, and the entire congregation end up damaged.

Fiscal malfeasance often occurs in similar ways. To misappropriate the congregation's money for personal gain can begin with nickels and dimes. No one will notice. But before long, it is dollars and tens and then even more. Such betrayal is a painful announcement that this ministry is in quadrant III. Likewise, many of the other ways that clergy "act out" to gain attention are flagrant cries of hopelessness. Judicatory executives tell me that they spend 80 to 90 percent of their time dealing with troubled clergy who are acting out the most; minor acting out gets ignored. And what usually happens in response to the acting out is either some small, corrective reprimand that gets things temporarily back on track or another instance of involuntary termination.

Steven McKinley speaks from the isolation of quadrant III when he states, "I hope that you'll feel a little less lonely out there on the mission field of ministry There's a lot of pain in the parish, and we share in and make it our pain. There is an inherent loneliness in the parish ministry."[6] Loneliness breeds a hunger for attachment, fulfillment, and satisfaction. And when that is not met constructively, as in quadrant I, then one tends to meet it destructively, as in quadrant III.

When I meet with clergy, their favorite activity is to complain about their congregations. There's even a game of "Would you believe" that clergy play, seeing if they can outdo each other in sharing outrageous events from current or past ministries. It is great sport to make fun of the painful reality that we clergy see no way of escaping. Yet it also reveals a systemic reality that permeates the church and appears to have no avenue for evasion. It is a disease that is reinforced time and time again at every level. When human beings hungry for affirmation realize that the only way to get that is to be the resident martyr/victim, to rescue everyone else at the price of their own well-being, to sacrifice, to endure, and to never complain, what hope can remain?

Movement to Interdependence

In the congregation, generally everything orbits around the clergy, especially in the pastor-centered church, as noted at the beginning of this chapter. The volume of responsibilities dumped on the clergy is inordinate, and because we clergy are so codependent, we accept that burden, rescue the laity from their responsibilities, and suffer the consequences. Were we to set healthy boundaries, accept only a reasonable amount of responsibility for the success of the ministry, and either delegate the rest or simply let it fail, the system would be broken. However, as has been attested already, this will not gain us our pats on the back and will only heap upon us the wrath of the congregation and the accusation that we are not carrying the load they expect us to carry.

We have choices. They may not be easy choices, but they are our choices. One very human choice is to take the frustration and resentment that comes from dwelling in quadrant IV and turn that on the congregation by moving to quadrant II. That kind of grandiose exercise usually fails and turns out to be more costly than one desires.

Another choice is to turn the frustration and resentment and blame onto ourselves by moving to quadrant III. It won't get us fired, but it will make life miserable for us and for those around us. It will impair our ministries. Depressed clergy are not effective clergy. Isolated clergy are void of the joy and energy that ministry requires. Depleted clergy have nothing to give.

Roy Oswald of the Alban Institute talks about a concept he calls the "vitality bucket."[7] It's a great metaphor, which I portray like this: One of the essential duties of the clergy is to show up every day in their ministry with a bucketful of vitality. In this way, they can dispense vitality to all those in need and thus infuse the ministry with life and energy. If the life of the clergy is totally enmeshed in the life of the congregation, however, then clergy have no external opportunity to refill the bucket. If the clergyperson is working seventy or more hours a week with only one day off—and that one day is consumed with chores and errands and the like—then there is no way to bring fresh and new vitality into the congregation. Likewise, if clergy do not use all their vacation days every year (which should be no less than twenty-four days per year) or their continuing education days (no fewer than twelve), then they are not refilling that bucket adequately. The clergy will be forced to drain vitality from within the congregation in order to refill their buckets so that they can fulfill that obligation of providing vitality to others. In the end, the clergy is merely one more empty bucket siphoning off life and energy from the ministry. Thus the clergyperson becomes a negative factor and not a positive one. To be that positive factor that brings a bucketful of vitality into the ministry regularly, the clergy must go outside the boundaries of the congregation to get a life that is rich in joy, love, inspiration, activity, affirmation, and hope—to fill that bucket to the brim with vitality. That is the only method that ultimately makes sense. It is the movement from quadrant IV to quadrant I.

For most clergy, there will be one particular key to making this move and turning the corner toward health. For me, the key was getting control of my calendar. When my son said, "So long, Dad. Thanks for stopping by," I made a commitment to claim at least one full day and two evenings a week. Those belonged to me and my family, and not the congregation. Likewise, I used all my vacation days and continuing education days. These were essential if I was going to keep my vitality bucket full.

We have choices. Some are very human and destructive. Only one ultimately makes sense, yet it is one that will not be encouraged but discouraged. The movement from quadrant IV to quadrant I will be considered selfish and a sign of disloyalty to the congregation and a lack of dedication. Good clergy work 24/7—that's the ticket to those pats on the back. But it is also the fast track to personal and congregational destruction.

THE INSTITUTIONALIZATION OF CODEPENDENCE

To come full circle, in order to face the reality of codependence and burnout among clergy, we must take a hard look at the institution in which these phenomena are nurtured. Let me be blunt: The church, especially in its pastor-centered form, propagates this disease, which some practitioners call an addiction. Moreover, this disease has become so pervasive within the system that it spreads from the highest denominational levels down to the people in the pews; indeed, it has become institutionalized. At its worst, the church seduces its victims into this addictive disease with the promise of a holy mission that should certainly create a system exempt from such flaws.

Those are tough words that will cause many deep discomfort, if not offense. How dare I criticize the church? It is God's sacred institution. How can something designed to serve God be so toxic?

This was part of my personal agony. How could I criticize what was supposed to be holy? How could I challenge an institution so enormous and so ancient that people believed it was an embodiment of the divine? Am I wrong? Or could it be that the system is truly diseased?

This is the church—Christ's body in our world. Therefore, hope exists. Hope can prevail. In the church, we have resources that do make a difference.

5

HOLINESS
AND SPIRITUALITY

In a book called *The Dynamics of Religion*, Bruce Reed and the Grubb Institute in England reported on research they conducted on what happens to people when they go to church—in particular, the Anglican Church.[1] Reed distilled his findings into what he calls a "theory of oscillation."

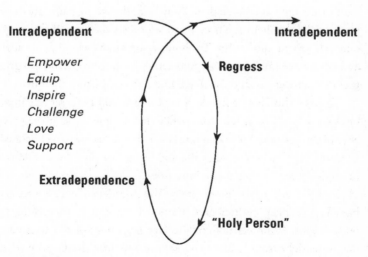

Theory of oscillation

UNDERSTANDING THE THEORY OF OSCILLATION

One of Reed's discoveries is that all week long, laypeople are in a state called *intradependence*. This means that they must manage their own chaos and confusion, discern the meaning of their existence and the purpose of life, find the path of right and wrong and struggle to follow that right path, keep themselves safe from harm, and find all the difficult answers to tough ethical questions like the death penalty, homosexuality, abortion, and the rest. Internally, they seek to manage their day-to-day lives in keeping with a deep sense of how they have been taught to live those lives. It is demanding and draining. They come to the church exhausted from a week's worth of such intense effort.

When laypeople enter the church, they can regress into a state we call *extradependence*, whereby they can lay down the melancholy burden of intradependence and rest for a while. In church, they can transfer that awesome responsibility to an external entity who will accept the burden with grace and honor. This external entity is the resident *holy person*. This holy person will know how to make a way through the chaos and confusion of everyday life and be able to direct them to the path that is right and guide them away from the wrong path. The holy person will keep them safe from harm, especially the harm that the evil one seeks to cast upon them. The holy person knows why they are alive and what is the purpose of life. And certainly, the holy person can give them the answers to all those tough questions that haunt their lives.

To go to church is to find a time of respite and to be set free from one's daily burdens, at least for a while. It is a time to be in the presence of the holy and know that one is safe. It is a chance to be liberated from the expectations of adult life and be free to embrace a childlike dependence on the holy for an hour or two.

I use the term *regress* intentionally. This extradependence is a retreat back to a familiar spiritual and emotional space. It is a returning to one's origins. Who was it from the very beginning of our lives who taught us right from wrong, who kept us safe from harm, who tried to direct us in the right path through life, who understood all the deep issues of life and their existential meanings, who gave us the answers to all our questions? Our parents. To go to church is to regress to that blessed innocence like a child in the presence of the holy that will give to us again the guidance, safety, and encouragement that we got from our parents. It is to be immersed into a state of grace and unconditional love that we knew as infants in our parent's arms. Only now, in church, the pastor—the holy person—has taken the place of the parent.

I read Reed's book at the time I was serving a congregation in a city where IBM was the largest employer of my parishioners, which meant that a large percentage of the church were research and development engineers. They were highly skilled, intelligent, and competent people who worked with an elevated level of expectations on the job. The number-two employer of the members of the congregation was the local university; again, these were learned and accomplished people who also performed at high standards on a daily basis. Yet when they came to church, those same highly competent people would often behave like children, treating me like some kind of parent figure who was there to do for them what, as mature adults, I thought they should be doing for themselves.

To regress back to this state of *dependence* on the holy for comfort and renewal, for safety and guidance, for inspiration and empowerment is exactly what is supposed to happen. As Jesus says in Mark 10:15, "Truly I tell you, whoever does not receive the kingdom of God as a little child will never enter it." Periodic regression from intradependence to an external dependence on the holy is exactly what God desires. To return to God with a spiritual and emotional emptiness that makes room in our hearts and souls for the presence of God to enter and enhance our sorry souls is a good thing.

The Holy Person

But from where did this concept of a *holy person* come? It is, in fact, as old as civilization itself. If confronted with two tribes of cave people, one savage and one civilized, how could one tell which is which? The civilized tribe had a holy person, a shaman. This holy person was a necessity for a tribe to be considered civilized. The job of the holy person was to know all the ancient stories containing the timeless truths that answer the existential questions, the truths that point the direction to the right path in life. The holy person was expected to have all the answers to the tough questions of life; in fact, the original holy people were thought to have the power over life and death. They were the healers to whom people went when they were sick. Although today we have mostly separated that duty and given it to the medical profession, modern holy people are still regarded as maintaining power over eternal life and death, heaven or hell.

The holy person in the tribe was not at the center about which all tribal life orbited; that place fell to the chief. Rather, the place for the holy person was out on the fringe of the tribe. The holy person was very different from everyone else in the tribe. No one else needed to be as holy. No one else needed to be in touch with the divine and a representative of the holy. Only one person needed to fulfill that responsibility. And whoever married a holy person could not be profane; that would be unthinkable. Only someone with reasonable holiness of their own would be worthy to share the residence of the holy person.

The Clergyperson as Holy Person

I was once told of a clergyman who served in a town near a university. His wife would go to the university for a graduate class one night a week. As the weeks went by, during the class breaks, the students got to know one another better. After several weeks, the fellow students asked the wife what her husband did for a living. "My husband is a parish pastor," she replied. The other students responded, "Oh, we thought you were *normal.*" Holy people aren't "normal." They're different—which means that they can be treated differently from everyone else. And not just the holy person and their spouse but also their children. Truly, the offspring of a holy person cannot be profane. They must also be to some extent holy—even if they're adopted and cannot be assumed to have inherited that holiness by genetics! If this is the case, then it is only logical that the other members of the tribe can put expectations of holiness on the clergy family that no other individuals in the tribe need to duplicate. No one else is held to the same standards of purity, compassion, dedication, or even availability.

The clergy represent God. As God is pure, compassionate, and always available, so must be the clergyperson. And as God would surely never turn God's back on the needs of the people, God's representative dare not either. The holy person must be on duty every hour, every day. The holy person dare not say no. The tribe needs the holy person to comply with those exceptional standards or its safety and security are threatened.

Even in our post-Christian society, where many feel no personal need for the church themselves, these same people often insist that the church remain and provide holy people for the sake of the community and its well-being. Holy people are essential and can be held responsible for the wellness and safety of the community in addition to its spiritual enrichment and emotional stability.

FROM EXTRADEPENDENCE TO INTRADEPENDENCE

We have not finished the oscillation; we are only halfway around the curve. To keep people in this extradependent state is to keep them attached to the holy person in an ongoing way. This is an addiction of its own kind. It is the kind of toxic religion that establishes a personality cult around the holy person, which is neither God's intent nor healthy.

Rather than keeping them in that extradependent state, it is the task of the holy person to inspire, equip, empower, love, support, and challenge the parishioners to return to their daily lives—to pick up their intradependence and change the world. Changing the world is not the duty of the holy person. Rather, the oscillation is complete when the holy person enables the parishioners to go back into real life and live in a new way that is consistent with the faith that will be a powerful force for change in the world.

This means that the worship experience should build to some climax that helps accomplish that enabling. The message and the liturgy should be filled with elements that communicate the tools members need to be bold and brave enough to truly live their faith in a hostile culture that is no longer—if it ever was!—Christian.

FROM EXTRADEPENDENCE TO CODEPENDENCE

The relevance of this discussion is obvious. If such high expectations are fair game for the members to place on the clergy, then no wonder an environment of codependence has evolved. One can see why "spiritual children" would treat the clergy like a parent and thus behave in ways that are juvenile and improper for normal adults; to some degree, the dynamics of the theory of oscillation condone such behavior. To see the holy person as chief enabler, family hero, rescuer, and cheerleader is patent. To add the role of scapegoat is no stretch. Who will get blamed when things go wrong? The holy person, who is there to appease the holy and protect the tribe from evil.

Once they are captured in the role of a holy person, the actual individual disappears as a mere mortal and begins to assume the role of the lost child. All the standard roles of codependence are inherent in this theory of oscillation, which is to say, we shouldn't be surprised that it has happened. Since this oscillation has been a part of every civilization from the beginning of time, it is not likely that it will just go away any time soon. It is as embedded in our culture as are all the other dynamics of codependence.

Guilty Guses (NFs) will feel the emotional pressure to keep people safe, to help them in times of need, and will feel guilty if the people are disappointed. Gotta Be Rights (NTs) will strive to rise to the level of expectations for fear of their appearing incompetent. By the Books (SJs) will seek to preserve such a long-standing tradition and will be very reluctant to defy it.

FROM CODEPENDENCE TO INTRADEPENDENCE

There is a way out. As the members mature in their faith, as they deepen their experience and understanding of the holy, they will become less and less dependent on an external source for that renewal and refreshment. As their prayer life is enriched and their spirituality strengthened, they will be able to find more and more of that holiness that God desires for them wherever they are. It is always at the ready. God is accessible at all times and in all places. As people grow in the faith and deepen their understanding of the ways of God, they will be better able to enter that state of extradependence in their own meditation and prayer, in their efforts of community service and evangelism, in their daily walk through life. That is the ultimate goal of the spiritual life—to have that inner confidence and empowerment that is not dependent on any other human being.

One source defines the signs and symptoms of inner peace as follows:

1. A tendency to think and act spontaneously rather than on fears based on past experiences.
2. An unmistakable ability to enjoy each moment.
3. A loss of interest in judging self.
4. A loss of interest in judging others.
5. A loss of interest in conflict.
6. A loss of interest in interpreting the actions of others.
7. A loss of ability to worry (this is a very serious symptom).
8. Frequent, overwhelming episodes of appreciation.
9. Contented feelings of connectedness with others and nature.
10. Frequent attacks of smiling through the eyes of the heart.
11. Increasing susceptibility to love extended by others as well as the uncontrollable urge to extend it.
12. An increasing tendency to let things happen rather than to make them happen.[2]

As clergy, we are not, never have been, and never will be holy people. While I have been ordained for nearly fifty years, I have not spent even one second of one day as a truly perfect and pure holy person. To assume that identity is close to heresy. Instead, our calling as clergy is to be conduits for God's holiness that it might flow through us on to

God's people. We serve in a *holy office*. My ordination papers say that I am ordained into the "Holy Office of Word and Sacrament." It is the office that is holy, not the person. Our role is not to save the world but to empower, equip, and inspire others that they might be freed and emboldened to do that blessed task.

The theory of oscillation explained why my laypeople acted the way they did, why they treated me the way they did, why they treated my family the way they did, and what I am called to do in response. It was a truly enlightening moment in my ministry; indeed, it helped shape my ministry more than many other teachings that fail to touch the elements of human encounter—clergy and parishioner—that this theory of oscillation so dramatically define. This is where the action takes place: the interplay of human thoughts, intentions, and expectations.

Of course, parishioners will continue to expect outrageous things from us. They will look to us to rescue them time and time again or anticipate our ability to have the answers and show them the way. It has been that way for millennia and isn't going to change any time soon. But that is not an excuse. Remember, the journey from quadrant IV to quadrant I, from codependence to interdependence, does not involve our relationship with our parishioners. It is the way we treat ourselves, the boundaries we set for ourselves, the personal care and attention we give ourselves that matter. We do this not at the expense of our ministries; rather, we strive for good self-esteem and good self-care to enrich and enhance our ministries with our buckets full of vitality and our souls brimming with God's hope and love.

SOME SPIRITUAL ISSUES

So far I have been rather heavy on the behavioral sciences in our discussion, which are important to understand if we want to refill our vitality buckets. But to be full of God's love and hope, we must take time to look at some spiritual issues as well.

I have made repeated reference to denial. There is another aspect to that called *minimization*. Minimization is not the same as denial. Denial is refusing to admit what is real. To minimize is to admit something is real but to deny due credit to its impact or severity. Although I have heard judicatory executives and other consultants make reference to the problem of codependence in the church, they tend to minimize the issue, reporting, "Of course it is there, but since it is so pervasive, it must not be too significant." Such an argument is dangerous and has only perpetuated the disease.

In addition, there is *delusion*. Delusion means we believe something in spite of clear facts to the contrary, which means we can hear the facts, but we don't assign the proper meaning to them. Of course clergy work too many hours, get enmeshed in their ministries, and abandon the care of themselves and their families, but that's no big deal—or so we say. Denial to that extreme is delusional. It creates a reality that defies the facts.

So what does all this have to do with the spiritual? Consider Luke 7:40–47, particularly verse 47: "But the one to whom little is forgiven, loves little." Those in minimization, denial, or delusion forfeit the chance for deep and personal forgiveness. To admit to so little is to receive minimal forgiveness. To so stifle the flow of God's love and mercy to us is to bankrupt our own souls of a wealth of love that we could use to share with others.

In his classic book *Addiction and Grace*, Gerald May writes, "The risk, of course, is to my addictions; if I try to live in accord with grace, then I will be relinquishing the gods I have made of my attachments. Grace threatens all my normalities."[3] That last phrase jumps out at me: "Grace threatens all my normalities." When something becomes normal—as when 80 percent of clergy share the same behaviors and attitudes—it becomes especially hard to be set free from those attachments—that addiction, the codependence—and instead embrace the pure and liberating grace of God.

Martin Luther insisted that only when we are driven to our knees by the weight of our sinfulness can we ever begin to appreciate the magnitude of God's forgiveness and grace. In the same way, only when we have the courage to see that what has become normal in the practice of ministry (and has been normal for generations) is really a disease that needs a cure—only then can the cure begin.

My clinical experience taught me that one cannot cure what one refuses to diagnose. In spiritual terms, one cannot be liberated from an attachment one refuses to confess. Despite all God's efforts, we will cling to the attachment until we have the courage to admit it and the bravery to name it for what it is—a disease.

When the church blesses the disease and has condoned it for so long, it makes this movement to health all the more difficult. It is why, for some people, separating religion from spirituality is helpful. In *The Dysfunctional Church*, Michael Crosby states, "Religion *assumes* faith. Spirituality *manifests* faith. There is a big difference. Religion can be addictive; spirituality cannot."[4]

For example, NFs experience solitude as loneliness, which they deeply fear. That fear of loneliness then can lead to a pathological attachment to others—as hero or martyr—to avoid the pain of isolation. Addictive behaviors are preferred over alienation. But a positive spirituality, based on the richness and freedom of God's grace, can empower us to embrace solitude without fear.

To succumb to the allures of codependence, to seek our safety in the enmeshments of ministry and unhealthy boundaries, is to deny the grace we have from God and strive to achieve our own salvation through the disease. We falsely believe that if we are loved/affirmed enough (NFs) or competent enough (NTs) or dutiful enough (SJs), then all will be right with us and with our souls. It is a false assumption. It is not of God. It detracts us from the true grace that is free and unconditional. Void of that grace, we fall prey to our fears of abandonment (NFs) or enmeshment (NTs) or chaos (SJs) and live without the courage we need to face these erroneous hopes and name them for what they are.

Faith that is not active in the courageous manifestation of its true convictions is not faith at all. To seek salvation in human relationships, competency, or tradition is wrong. These are not the convictions of God. This is not to say that human relationships or competency or tradition are evil in themselves; they are only evil when they become an attachment of their own and replace our primary attachment, which ought to be with God, in trust, bathed in God's grace.

Empowered by that grace, we can have the courage to name and claim our disease. Empowered by that grace, we can have the courage to name and claim the disease propagated by the church. Empowered by that grace, we can dare to address and even attack the forces of our culture that continue to feed and nourish this disease throughout our society. Empowered by that grace, we can be bold enough to swim against the tide, oppose the forces of our culture, and be the vanguard of the counterculture movement that is now so desperately needed.

* * *

This completes our discussion of the dynamics of codependence. Before moving on to part 2, which focuses on components in the recovery process, I encourage you to fill out the personal assessment in appendix 1, which will help you understand where you currently are relative to these issues and grasp which elements described in part 2 will be most helpful to your situation.

Part Two

HOPE AND HEALING

6

BECOMING GOSPEL-CENTERED

In part 2 of this book on clergy burnout and codependence, I will explore various components in the recovery process. As I do so, I invite you to look at each of these components as an item at a smorgasbord. Some of the items will (and should) apply to you immediately; others can be embraced later. Some may not apply to your situation at all. Be careful in dismissing any one item, however; it may be just the one you need, even if it initially makes you uncomfortable or confused. Remember, codependence has been with us a long time; it will not be controlled or eliminated easily. Recovery is a long and often tedious process that requires many trials and enduring effort. Often discomfort and even some brief disorientation accompany the most important work in this process. Therefore, I reiterate: Select from the following chapters what you need, then work it and work it well. Then return to another chapter and see what else you can embrace on your road to recovery. As the saying goes, "It's possible to swallow an elephant—just one bite at a time, not all at once."

THE FOUR ELEMENTS OF THE GOSPEL

Part 1 ended with a brief discussion of spiritual issues related to codependence. In the same fashion, any recovery process needs to begin with one's spiritual roots, to address one's belief system and its impact on one's life. For the Christian, this means going to the gospel and exploring its fundamental parts. (Although the following may reveal my Lutheran theological biases, I believe that a broad cross section of Christians will resonate with the insights I share.) For anything to be gospel requires four essential elements. This means that all four are necessary, not just one or two.

Good News

First, gospel is always good news—that is what the word *gospel* means. Gospel cannot be bad news. Some characterize statements like the following as gospel: "If you don't, you are going to hell." That cannot be gospel because it is not good news. Such a statement is, rather, a proclamation of the law. God's law is a good thing, as the Scriptures repeatedly attest. We need God's law for the functioning of civilizations, to help us discern our own sinfulness, and to keep us in line. But we dare not confuse law with gospel.

The good news is the pronouncement that Jesus was born, lived, taught, healed, and then died and conquered death *for us*! Probably those two last words are the most difficult to believe—that the one holy and almighty God has done all of this, not for all of humanity as some kind of blanket solution, but for each and every individual, personally, intimately, and lovingly. In person, Jesus delivers each of us from the consequences of our sins and liberates us from all our addictions, including our addiction to sin. One to one, heart to heart, Christ seeks a personal relationship with each human being to inform our lives and empower us with hope.

That is the first essential part of the gospel.

Hope

Second, gospel is always a message of hope, never a message of threats, shame, blame, anger, intimidation, disgrace, or punishment. Gospel does empower me to own my own spiritual poverty—that is, the truth that we all stand before God in need. None of us is worthy of God's grace and forgiveness. We are all addicted to sin, and we cannot free ourselves. So we come to God with our spiritual pockets empty; we are poor and in need of God's forgiveness and redemption and of the riches of faith.

Owning our spiritual poverty is liberating. It means that we don't have to measure up to some arbitrary standard of perfection. It means knowing full well that one has never and will never do enough of whatever it is one is supposed to do for the Lord. Whether it be believing, serving, giving, loving, telling, or whatever, not one of us will ever do it as much as one should to be fair to the God who so generously gave it to us. Our salvation is worth more than any of us can ever repay. *Enough* needs to be a key word in our spiritual vocabularies, for it reminds us that to embrace spiritual poverty is to affirm one's absolute dependence on God's mercy and grace.

At the same time, hope liberates us from shame. Shame is quite different from guilt. Shame says, "I *am* wrong"; guilt says, "I *did* wrong." There is a world of difference. Spiritual poverty has nothing to do with shame. Shame and hope cannot dwell together. Guilt, however, is compatible with spiritual poverty. Having pockets that are empty before God is one's own fault; it means not doing whatever it is that God desires one to do. For that failure of action, each of us is guilty.

But at the very same time, God affirms each of us as God's child, loved from the beginning and cherished so much that Jesus died and rose again on our behalf. There can be no shame for a Christian. Shame is a denial of Christ's passion. Without Christ, we are lost. With Christ's passion, we can be proud to claim our positions within the household of God—despite our spiritual poverty.

Being who we really are—sinners in need of redemption yet filled with the hope of salvation—is safe. Since there is no limit to God's hope, we can constantly be confident in its more than adequate supply for our lives, regardless of all our pain and sorrows, suffering and woes. Nothing can be so great or overwhelming that God's hope will not match. In that hope, there are no false promises or empty dreams. It is a reality born of the cross and empty tomb. It is the "real thing" on which we can place all our hopes and dreams from now until eternity.

Unconditional Love

The third essential element of the gospel is that it is always a message of unconditional love. By that, I mean two things. First, it means that God loves us without condition. There is no "if–then" to God's love. There is no "if you will do, then I will love you." We humans make good service of that; too many marriages and relationships are composed of such an arrangement. After all, if–then is good business. It strikes a bargain by which both parties can benefit, but it has nothing to do with the gospel. Instead, the gospel clearly states that God's love is ours *regardless*. There are no conditions placed on receiving the love so freely given by God. Even the most despicable person on the face of God's earth is not so disgusting that God cannot love that individual. That's the scope and magnitude of God's love. It is without any condition.

At the same time, God's love is beyond all conditions. To say "I love you" is to make a promissory declaration: "I promise to give you my love." All such promissory statements on the face of this earth have at least three conditions. Let me explain.

When I do a workshop, I demonstrate this point by promising that at the end of the workshop, I will give each participant a fifty-dollar bill. However, I let them know that there are three conditions to that promise, the first being my sincerity. Am I sincere, or am I just pretending? Well, I am sincere. I would find real pleasure in passing out fifty-dollar bills.

But the second condition to my promise has to do with my capability. Am I standing there with a wallet full of fifty-dollar bills? *I wish it were true!* I do not have such wealth, but let's make believe that I do. Therefore, I am sincere and I am capable.

The final condition is that I am still alive at the end of the workshop. The likelihood is exceedingly high that I will be alive, but there is always the possibility that I may have a fatal heart attack, an insane person might break in and shoot me dead, or a meteor might fall on my head. While none of those is likely to happen, it could. I am not beyond these three conditions. Therefore, the final condition on all human promises is death.

But when Jesus promises to love us forever, first of all, we know that Jesus is sincere. How do we know? Because he already died and conquered death for us. That's a rather bold and dramatic statement of sincerity. Such a person we can trust.

Is Jesus capable? Of course he is. While fully human, Jesus is also fully divine. Jesus is part of the Holy Trinity; he is God and is therefore capable of anything. Walk on water, heal the sick, change water into wine—you name it, Jesus can do it.

And finally, the ultimate condition on every promise—death. Will death intervene and stop Jesus from loving us? Impossible. Jesus now exists on the *other side of death*. Death is no longer in his future. That is the critical difference between resurrection and resuscitation. If Jesus had been merely resuscitated like Lazarus, then Jesus would still have death somewhere in his future, and his promise would be so conditioned. But now that Jesus has conquered death and lives fully on the other side of death, it can no longer interfere with all the promises made by Jesus. Death has no power over Jesus.

So the third essential part of the gospel is unconditional love—both without conditions and beyond conditions.

An Open Future

The final essential part of the gospel is an open future. Earlier I mentioned the law, which is a wonderful thing that we need. But it does not liberate us; rather, it constrains us, as it should. The law repeatedly says, "Thou shalt not . . ." Over and over again, the law boxes us in for our own good. But not so the gospel. The gospel does truly liberate us to love and do what seems appropriate. Jesus taught, "I give you a new commandment, that you love one another. Just as I have loved you, you also should love one another" (John 13:34).

Let me illustrate it this way: The law says, "Thou shalt not steal." But if my friend were starving to death and I had no money, what would I do? I would go to the grocery store and beg for food for my starving friend. If the grocery store refused to give me food, then love would compel me to steal food so that my friend would not starve to death. Better that I go to jail for theft than that my friend dies of starvation. Love so compels.

The open future of the gospel is that dynamic. There are no limits to what love might lead us to do so long as it is within the confines of a genuine and deep love that is reflective of the ways of God. The gospel creates those open and unpredictable opportunities for which we need to be prepared. This does not mean confining ourselves to such a strict loyalty to tradition that anything new or different is unthinkable. To live in such a fashion is to deny the gospel as an active part of our lives. To say that nothing innovative can occur in our worship or in how we function as the church is to deny the gospel.

God is full of surprises. Tradition serves a wonderful purpose, but it can stand in the way of the gospel. For instance, I love traditional worship, but when I make of it an attachment, then I have forfeited the gospel and embraced an addiction in its place. Moreover, I deny the freedom of God to do something new.

The Christian church now exists in a post-Christian era. That is, Christianity at its best no longer plays a significant role in shaping our culture. To be a genuine Christian today is to participate in a counterculture movement. Many of the old ways need to be tested; they were not designed for such a counterculture era. The old ways were born out of a time of Christian dominance, or at least of a somewhat favored status. Christianity and culture had an allegiance that worked for both. This is not so today. The old ways that reflected that past understanding may no longer fit our current situation and challenge. The good news of an open future gives us the freedom to respond to our day and age in a new way that is fully appropriate to the purposes of God.

THE GOSPEL AND RECOVERY FROM CODEPENDENCE

When a clergyperson seeks to find their way into recovery for codependence, the beginning point is making the gospel the center of one's life. This means endeavoring to live and give *good news*, *hope*, *unconditional love*, and an *open future* to oneself and to others. All of this grounds us spiritually in a place where there is firm footing and lasting stability. It liberates us. It frees us to stop seeking perfection and to embrace our spiritual poverty. It affirms one's status as a member of the household of God purely by God's grace. It affords a love that is both without and beyond all conditions. It sets us free to enjoy the traditions of the church where appropriate or to change them where love dictates.

The gospel is the anchor of our existence. Without it, we drift into chaos, void of hope. In the tempest of breaking an addiction, in the torment of detaching from an attachment, we need a source, a power stronger than ourselves, to sustain that effort. The gospel of Jesus and all Christ's love, mercy, and grace are that source, that power that cannot be found in such a reliable form anyplace else. When we know and feel the pressures that this spiritual freedom ignites, returning to the faith that brought us into a relationship with God at the beginning is the spiritual movement the gospel inspires. In trust, we can dare to find the strength to break free from addiction and stand at a safe distance from all our pathological attachments.

7

DEVELOPING
SPIRITUAL MATURITY

A second key element in recovering from the effects of codependence and burnout is developing spiritual maturity. To explore this topic, I will trace the spiritual movement of the disciples of Jesus as recorded in the New Testament. The following graph provides a quick and simple overview of this movement:

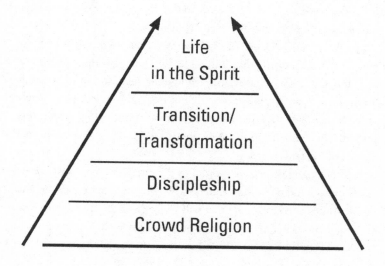

CROWD RELIGION

The disciples were called from the crowd. The beginning point in our spiritual journey to maturity begins with our place in the crowd. The New Testament records large groups who gathered to hear the teachings of Jesus, to receive the blessings of his healing touch, or to be "entertained" with his novel ideas. The Gospel writers report that packs of four or five thousand men (or maybe as many as twenty thousand, including women and children!) assembled for Jesus's presentations.

The crowd makes no commitment. Their level of maturity is minimal. They are like children gathering at the feet of a storyteller. They may be moved in the moment, but as that moment passes, so does their inspiration and commitment. The New Testament tells us only of a fickle mob who cheers at one instance and then cries for Jesus's death at another. The crowd is not a place for the movement of the Spirit. It is only when we dare to come forward out of the throng and make a personal response to the call of Jesus that we take any serious steps on the path to spiritual maturity. Spiritual maturity is not a group event; it is an individual endeavor. No one can do it for us, nor can the energy of the crowd replace our own inner churnings.

Jesus welcomes the crowd. Apparently, he has no problem with the meager maturity of the multitude. He does not condemn them as he does those in religious leadership who guide the innocent ones astray. So the crowd gathers, is temporarily inspired, gets healed, or is merely entertained. Then they disperse without their spirits being significantly moved. They remain uninformed about holy matters and the deeper aspects of the faith journey.

In how many ways have we sought the safety of the crowd? We do not want to stand out and be different. We do not dare to speak up and say what may need to be said that will likely spark the crowd's disfavor. Go along and get along. Hide and be safe. That is the temptation the crowd offers us.

Nevertheless, from the crowd, a few came who dared to make a serious commitment to follow this itinerant preacher, Jesus. They dared to dedicate themselves to his teachings and changed their lives dramatically. They became different people—different from the crowd. Although their understandings are yet quite simple and naïve, they nevertheless have taken a profound step away from the ways of the world, away from the common and ordinary values and principles of daily living, and dared to seek a new way of living according to the teachings of Jesus. They have voluntarily turned their backs on the "old ways"—even the old ways of their religion—and taken the risk of embracing new ways to know God, to worship, and to live. "Lord, teach us how to pray . . ."

I call this the movement into the next step, discipleship. From crowd religion, some dare to act on what they hear from Jesus, take it to heart, and make it their new way of life. It is just that—a first step, not the final step. That is, while movement from the crowd into discipleship is admirable, it is not the end. It is tempting to assume that our childhood experiences of Sunday school and confirmation gave us all we need to know about the faith. Why bother with further learning? We have the basics. What more do we need?

Stifling the maturity process by denying it the fresh air of new insights and knowledge is another attachment that ensnares us. Youth drop out after confirmation; adults feel no need for Christian education. And even clergy fail to pursue continuing education with a proper fervor and delight. All of us fall short in our passion for understandings beyond the simplistic, the dichotomies of right and wrong, and the shallow answers fit for a child but not for one mature in the faith.

DISCIPLESHIP

One problem with some of our religious traditions is that they assume that the step forward into discipleship is the final step. All that remains for spiritual maturity are some refinements, some fine-tuning, and then going out to recruit others for the same exercise. There is no agenda for the spiritual life after conversion.

The disciples were not far into their maturity, and it showed in their petty squabbles about who would get to sit where in the kingdom. It showed in their naïve expectations that Jesus would fight some fierce battle against the Roman soldiers or some other nonsense that really had nothing to do with what Jesus taught at all. The disciples were shallow in their faith. Energetic, yes, but energy and excitement do not mean maturity. It is great to move into discipleship, to discover a new way of living that has promise and a hope that is eternal. It is yet another thing to appreciate fully the depth of that promise and the magnitude of the hope God provides. Much of the Christian life is experienced in that naïve, innocent way. Simplistic, like children in Sunday school, the disciples had basic answers for issues that are far more than basic—issues of profound substance and depth.

But discipleship is wonderful and good. It works for some time. It enlivens us and begs us to learn more, to read our Bibles and explore the faith, even if all we want are fundamental answers—concrete, binary. Discipleship is a phase that is most comfortable reducing everything to that dichotomy: right and wrong, good and evil. Void of the gray that is often the deeper reality, discipleship dances in the garden of innocent and cursory knowledge.

Unfortunately, discipleship cannot endure in the long haul. If we take the risk of being truly honest with ourselves, discipleship will eventually break down in two ways. First, from without. Even if we have a firm belief that we are now different, that we now live by higher standards, that we are purer, more righteous, and all that goes with it—the world won't give two hoots. Interacting with the mundane, we expect to be treated in a new way as we experience the new life: "No, no; I'm not like everyone else. You can trust me. My word is sincere and good. I'm one of the 'good people' who follow Jesus." But the world will pay no attention. So we are dismissed and do not understand why. Our joy and confidence are challenged and can fade in the face of the cold, hard realities of the mundane.

Second, discipleship also breaks down from within. When we have the courage to take a good hard look at ourselves, to examine our lives more closely, to test how "pure and good" we actually are, we come to a painful and harsh truth: we are by nature sinful and unclean, "for all have sinned and fall short of the glory of God" (Rom 3:23).

That's as true for the disciple as it is for everyone else, yet here is where some denial can surface. It is too painful for many disciples to acknowledge the extent of their sinfulness: "No, no; I gave my life to Christ. I no longer sin as I did before."

Perhaps, but it is more likely that the disciple simply has found new and creative ways to betray God's teachings.

In the New Testament, this becomes evident in the garden of Gethsemane. Jesus is betrayed by one of the disciples. And when faced with the ultimate test of loyalty, every one of the disciples flees. Betrayal and abandonment were the testaments of those first disciples who had the great benefit of a firsthand encounter with Jesus. If they were no more devout than this, then what should we expect for ourselves?

In the hard tests, the most elemental temptations, we often fail, betray, and abandon all that we proclaim when times are easy. Life is difficult. There are no simple paths through our days and years. It is a struggle. Sometimes we win; more often than not, we fall prey to the skills of the evil one. That's why Jesus had to die for us. On our own, we cannot achieve perfection. Remember the word *enough*? Well, guess what?

TRANSITION/TRANSFORMATION

In the garden, faced with the ultimate test, the disciples fled. At that point, they had to enter a new stage of spiritual maturity that I call transition or transformation (either term works well). It is a time of deeper spiritual awakening. It is not a joyful time but a time of bitter awareness of the measure of our failures. It is the disillusion of our naïveté. It is the harsh realization that our simplistic, binary, concrete answers to life's very complex problems just don't work. It is a time of painful coming to terms with the truth that we don't have the wisdom we thought we had, and we have really just begun in this pilgrimage to spiritual maturity. For many, this is a point of dropping out: "Look, it doesn't work. As hard as I tried, I could not achieve the level of purity I desired. So just forget it. I'm out."

The church has not adequately understood this movement of the spiritual life and therefore is often unprepared to address this personal crisis. Fellow disciples will provide only superficial prescriptions that will be inadequate. Crowd religion folks will only shake their heads in a quandary. When all they get are the same old superficial answers, youth will drop out after confirmation, and adults will see no need for further education.

But for those who can affirm that this time of transition and transformation is in fact a gift, much promise unfolds. No, it is not fun to look in the mirror and see a sinner as flawed as ever. It is not uplifting to lay before ourselves the agony of our weaknesses and failures. But for those who dare to be so brave, God responds with a measure of grace and forgiveness even greater than the magnitude of our faults and failures—for God's mercy is infinite.

In transition/transformation, our main spiritual agenda is to attempt to gain some sense of improvement. We strive to be more like Jesus. We know our shortcomings, and we no longer seek to deny them. But we now desire a way to overcome those shortcomings and grow in faith and action so that we can more faithfully emulate the purity of Jesus. We can attest that we are both saints and sinners, worthy of condemnation yet redeemed. We can endure the imperfection knowing that we are on a journey and that perfection is not its true goal. The goal is faithfulness, not perfection. That is priceless learning.

This is what happened to the original disciples from the time in the garden until Pentecost. In the garden, they were confused and bewildered. Through the resurrection, they remained overwhelmed. At Pentecost, another step in the process of spiritual maturity began. From that point on, the disciples were so full of God's Spirit that they were even willing to lay down their lives for the Lord. Indeed, all of them would do just that—die a martyr's death rather than betray or abandon again.

LIFE IN THE SPIRIT

The final stage, which I call life in the Spirit, is marked by an intense and deep sense of God's peace so profound as to be beyond description. In life in the Spirit, there is a quiet joy, unlike the noisy joy of discipleship. This quiet joy is a feeling at the very center of our souls that all is well, despite the chaos and pain of the world. All is well because God is in charge, not us. All is well because we do not need to rescue everyone, only do our fair share. All is well in the sense that there is a oneness with nature and with others that creates a bond, a harmony that births a tranquility and a release. All is well because we have come to terms with a reality that is greater than anything this world could propose. All the agendas of this world fall short. Only God's agenda rings true. And God's agenda is beyond our power to fully comprehend. Ours is not to have all the answers; ours is to be faithful to the quest.

In life in the Spirit, there is a profound surrender. It is a surrender to the majesty of God. It is a surrender to a life of devout service, witnessing as we are able, actively seeking justice and peace for all people, and yet free to be just who we are. As an energized agent of God's redemption, we pledge our lives to the work of healing and renewal for all people, especially those who cannot advocate for themselves: the poor, the hopeless, the forgotten and forlorn, the very young, the very old.

Life in the Spirit also hungers for community, the fellowship of believers. Those in this level of spiritual maturity know they cannot go it alone; the demands of life are too overwhelming. Even with their advanced level of inner peace, they still seek the company and companionship of others in the faith. Likewise, the worship life of the church is essential for them to sustain this mature blessing.

Two well-known and recent examples of this life in the Spirit would be Mother Teresa and Martin Luther King Jr. Both made enormous statements with the way they lived their lives: Mother Teresa's quiet witness echoed throughout the world, while Dr. King's testimony freed people all over the earth. Yet neither saw themselves as great or deserving. In that inner confidence, they found their strength.

Life in the Spirit is the ultimate goal of spiritual maturity. Yet as the examples of Mother Teresa and Dr. King attest, very few ever achieve it. Apparently, in God's economy, it is not necessary for the masses to be so advanced. It is like a pyramid, with the large numbers at the bottom. For instance, if you consider the thousands who may have gathered in crowds around Jesus, only a small number were called forth into discipleship. The New Testament records no more than about seventy who dared to follow Jesus in any significant way. And from those seventy, only twelve journeyed through transition/transformation into life in the Spirit.

What that means for us is that we are invited into a lifelong process that will have its movement both forward and backward. It is a dynamic process that calls us into an ever-deeper relationship with the holy. Again, the goal is not "passing the final exam," or "climbing to the top of the class," or any such achievement. The goal is merely to be faithful to the process, open to the Spirit's movement within us, and responsive to that movement in our actions with others. On our own, we cannot just decide to have life in the Spirit. Maturity is a gift. It is not ours to acquire, but only to receive. All we can do is be aware of the steps along the way and their various agendas and seek an openness to the Spirit's intentions.

SPIRITUAL LIFE SURVEY

I now invite you to inquire for yourself where you are in this journey to spiritual maturity. Although the following spiritual life survey is influenced by my Lutheran leanings, it should be no problem to read each item from your own faith tradition and make any necessary adjustments. I have made no attempt to make this "scientific" by any definition (after all, spiritual things are not scientific, so why try to force them into a discipline where they do not belong?). Rather, the purpose of this survey is twofold. First, it may assist you in gaining some fundamental understanding of the various characteristics of each step in the process of spiritual maturity and afford you a chance to discover where you are in that process. Second, this helps paint a picture of the process in a way that invites you to look at what lies ahead for you as you seek to enjoy a deeper faith and a closer relationship with the holy.

In completing the statements that follow, choose the response that best expresses how you really function (how you behave), not how you think you ought to function or what you should do or what would be ideal. Be completely honest! Select the response that best describes you.

Spiritual Life Survey

1. My approach to *life* is:
   a. Life gives you what it gives you; it's all a matter of circumstances. God plays no active part anymore. Live accordingly.
   b. If I obey and perform well, I will be rewarded; if I disobey, I will be punished. Keep in mind that "Ledger Book" in heaven.
   c. Life is a struggle filled with many challenges; it is a quest for a goal; a sense of being incomplete, a movement to fulfill the quest. Be better every day.
   d. Life is a gift from God; a privilege to be enjoyed, used for others, and celebrated. God made us for God's purpose. My life is lived accordingly.

2. My view of *afterlife* is:
   a. I'm not sure there is an afterlife—it doesn't really affect the way I live.
   b. A final judgment based on performance with reward or punishment; heaven or hell. I fear hell, so I live to get into heaven.
   c. A final appeal to God's Mercy; salvation by grace and not merit. I live trusting in the Lord, for I know I am a sinner.
   d. Something to be reckoned with seriously but not fearfully; a transition to being complete. I live in quiet joy and confidence.

3. When I *pray*, I see it as:
   a. I really do not pray regularly.
   b. An opportunity to place my concerns before God.

    c. Response "b" plus a striving for a closer relationship with Christ. Confession.

    d. Responses "b" and "c" plus celebrating the fullness of life; glorifying God. Giving praise and thanksgiving.

4. My ***view of the world*** is:

    a. I have no certain view of the world; OR my view is secular and not spiritual at all.

    b. Fairly optimistic; generally the good wins over the evil so that I live depending on my good deeds to really make a difference.

    c. Evil rules this earth and the good awaits final vindication (final recognition and reward) in God's Coming Kingdom. The world is to be patiently endured.

    d. The world is a temporal stage of tragedy and comedy, bad and good. It is a place to seek justice, to witness to the Gospel, to celebrate in quiet joy and confidence. So I live out that pursuit of justice for others. I am an active witness for God and I live in contentment and peace.

5. To me, "***social ministry***" is:

    a. Does that mean socializing? I'm not sure. Sounds like fun.

    b. Doing God's work out in the world as God ordains for us; being dutiful.

    c. Giving back to others since God has given so much to me, an unworthy sinner; being more like Jesus, compassionate, etc.

    d. A joy and delight; the privilege of being responsible to all God's people and God's creation; beyond duty, it is a pleasure.

6. To me, ***love*** is:

    a. I'm not sure OR I don't care OR I don't really think about it.

    b. Tenderness and warmth—a kind of romantic love shared between people.

    c. Self-sacrifice; Christ on the Cross. I live to give myself to others. Delayed gratification to benefit others.

    d. Building each other up; living to love again in a new way, more than self-sacrifice. A very deep sense of personal commitment, even unto death. Seeking community and genuine fellowship.

7. To me, *sin* is:

    a. I have no real idea; never thought much about it.

    b. Occasionally puzzling; means that I missed the mark somehow. I really am a good person who obeys God and does not do wrong very often.

    c. A power that is within me that wars against my good intentions. I know I am a sinner, though I struggle to be less sinful.

    d. Already defeated by Christ for me; yet I still have to wrestle with it, only now with a strong sense of confidence. I sin, for which I am sorry but I do not feel victimized by my sinfulness, thanks to God.

8. To me, *forgiveness* is:

    a. Not something I worry about or even think about very much.

    b. Something God gives me when I confess my sins; confession is something we all ought to do regularly even if we haven't done many things wrong.

    c. The great gift of God's mercy given to me, an unworthy sinner.

    d. Something I celebrate and do not take for granted; a deep awareness of some of the enormous magnitude of God's great love for me.

9. The *Holy Spirit* has *given me*:

    a. I really don't know; I'm not sure I care.

    b. A healthy nature ready to grow and develop. I am a believer who proudly obeys God.

    c. A new presence of God in my life; nurturing, supporting, confronting. I am not satisfied with my spiritual wayward-ness and the Spirit affirms and loves me as I struggle with my shortcomings.

    d. A new community of faith (the church); new life, freedom, purpose, strength. God active in my life, molding my life and guiding my decisions and actions. I have a deep and pro-found confidence in the guidance of the Spirit.

10. In my *faith life*, I would say I am:

    a. Faith is not my strong point. I am not sure what I believe or how my faith changes or shapes my life.

    b. Confident that I believe, yet knowing that there are moments of doubt. As a believer, the doubting confuses me; but by obeying God, I am put right again.

    c. Critical of myself. I need to lean on God. My faith life is an ongoing quest to be more like Christ.

    d. Mature, accepting, free; I am sure that all things really do work together for the good for all those who love God.

11. In my *relationships* with *other people*, I:

    a. Am like most people, not very different. It pays to be very careful in one's relationships. Don't get hurt.

    b. Follow the Golden Rule. I am a good person who treats people nicely and politely and people are usually nice to me.

    c. Am willing to practice self-denial; delayed gratification for the other's sake. In my quest to be a better person, being for others as Christ was for us is my goal.

    d. Accept suffering as a part of all human relationships; yet I still prefer working with others rather than going it alone.

12. As I see it, *my agenda* in life is:

    a. To earn money, seek security, have a nice family.

    b. To do good and avoid evil (reward and punishment so that I may go to heaven and not to hell). Obey God.

    c. To struggle to be authentic and true. To overcome my sinfulness.

    d. To be obedient to God's plan over any and every human plan; serving all people, because I love.

13. To me, *knowledge/understanding/truth* is:

    a. Whatever the world determines it to be.

    b. Information, data, facts, empirical; from the five senses; numbers, science.

    c. A growing sense of something beyond in tension with the empirical/factual/date. No longer satisfied with my own sense of knowing. Truth is to be pursued; a quest.

    d. Spiritual enlightenment rather than the empirical/factual; God's agenda over any/all human agendas. Worldly knowledge is not at all satisfactory.

14. As I experience it, the *Christian community* is:

    a. Confusing to me; I have never really experienced it.

    b. A hearty fellowship with those who try to do good.

    c. A mutual journey, sharing a common spirit, in quest of the truth.

    d. Believers bound solidly together in Christ's love and a mutual commitment to enhance each other for the sake of doing God's work.

15. I see *myself* as:

    a. I'm not sure of my self-image OR I see it in secular terms based on my vocation or financial status.

    b. A Child of God; I am trying to do good and avoid evil.

    c. Both saint and sinner; hopeless yet hopeful; adopted, saved by God's grace.

    d. An heir to God's Kingdom; an energized agent of redemption; one who seeks to be a healer in an ailing world.

16. Regarding my *self-worth*, I am:
    a. Measured by my worldly success, financial status, political power, popularity.
    b. Confident that I do more good than bad.
    c. Gaining confidence in God's acceptance and counting on God's forgiveness.
    d. Accepted and acceptable; granted purely by God's grace.

17. As I appreciate it, *baptism* is:
    a. Something you do; a nice ritual; it makes everyone feel good. I'm not sure it has any big meaning.
    b. An important first step to gain our acceptance into Heaven; Baptism and belief are the tickets to eternal life.
    c. A huge blessing God gives to me even though I am not worthy; the initial washing away of my sins.
    d. My identity; my "birthright" into God's Family in which I rejoice always in quiet confidence and contentment.

18. As I experience it, the *Lord's Supper (Holy Communion)* is:
    a. I never really think about it OR I am not sure OR I really don't care.
    b. A way to remember the past (Christ's death and resurrection) and a hope for victory in the future (heaven).
    c. The Real Presence of Christ's Body and Blood given to forgive my sins.
    d. Christ's Real Presence creating a new community of faith and love in mission. It pulls us together in the mystery and majesty of the sacrament and moves us to service for others.

19. As I live it, *God's love for me* is:
    a. Not something I think about very much. I guess it is there, but I don't spend much time dwelling on it.
    b. The fruit of my obedience; because I am a faithful servant of God, God bestows on me God's wonderful love.

    c. Something I do not deserve, but God gives to me out of God's mercy and grace; not something I take for granted; a blessing.

    d. The source of all my contentment and inner peace; something I know I can never fully imagine in its entirety or scope; it is more than I can ever comprehend; it is at the very depth of my being and empowers me, even when all else fails.

20. To me, **salvation** means:

    a. Who knows; that's one of those church words that I never fully understood.

    b. That I made it; I was faithful in doing what God expects me to do and I "passed the test."

    c. The miracle of God's grace given to me despite all my faults and failures; something I do not deserve.

    d. My identity; I am one whom God loves even as God loves all people; I do not think in terms of "who is saved or who is not saved"; for me all people are the joy of God's eye and the focus of God's unswerving attention and I treat them as blessed equals in the Kingdom.

21. To me, **church membership** means:

    a. I don't know, you go to church and pay your money and all of that.

    b. The *privilege* I have earned because of my faithfulness and obedience; I am entitled to certain benefits because I am a member of the congregation.

    c. Something I am allowed to have in spite of my sinfulness; something I am beginning to value and cherish more and more.

    d. A key part to my belonging to the Family of God; my spiritual family whom I have the pleasure of loving and supporting; the privilege of being responsible and doing all I can to further the Kingdom in joy and in quiet excitement.[1]

All the "a" responses reflect crowd religion. All the "b" responses reflect discipleship. All the "c" responses reflect transition/transformation. And all the "d" responses reflect life in the Spirit. It's that plain and simple. If you are like me, some aspects of my life are at one level, and others are at a different level. Regardless, where you are now is good. Remember, the goal is faithfulness, not achievement. At the same time, look at one level above where you are and pray for the Spirit to enable you to be blessed with that new characteristic of your spiritual life. Do not feel compelled. Instead, just remain open and desiring. The Spirit knows when and how. Surrender to the Spirit's sense of timing and what is best for you.

This survey also helps highlight several important points. First, we should not be so hard on ourselves. If Jesus could only call about seventy people from crowd religion into discipleship, what kind of "success" do we think we are going to have? For whatever reason, in God's economy, great masses of disciples are not necessary. This whole Christian movement was started with just a handful, and look what resulted. God does know best. So let's stop being so hard on ourselves when great hordes do not respond to our ministries or flock into seminary. Let's do our best and be done with it. Let's love the crowd, meet them where they are in their spiritual journeys (or lack thereof), and respond to them with patient care. Our task is to create an environment that is inviting and fertile for the Spirit's movement.

Second, we need to recognize where we are in our spiritual maturity and acknowledge the limitations of our own status. If we are in crowd religion, then we need to ask ourselves how much of an actual commitment have we made to our Lord. Perhaps we are so enmeshed with our codependence because we are using that to fulfill in us what a personal relationship with God might otherwise complete. Lacking that dynamic presence in our lives, we spend great energy creating other attachments that are pathological.

If we are in discipleship, as I suspect many are, then we can recognize that our simplistic knowledge has many gaps. Might we be attempting to close those gaps with codependent activity? Through poor boundaries and martyr/victim status, we can bluff our way into believing that we are great servants of the holy when we are not. Confusing the crowd with our grandiose pronouncements and eloquent declarations is not serving our Lord. Bluffing gets everyone nowhere. But coming to terms with that should not cause shame. Shame has nothing to do with God. Instead, the new awareness can afford us the rich opportunity to affirm where we are and pray for the Spirit to empower us to move ahead.

The temptation in discipleship is to re-create believers like ourselves. Since we think we have it all figured out, it would only make sense to duplicate this in others. This is loaded with classic elements of codependence and ripe with issues of control. It can lead us to quadrant II. It can also take us, in quadrant IV, to great lengths of suffering for the sake of the cause when all we are doing is living with weak boundaries and duplicating naïveté.

Those who are in transition/transformation may feel so deeply the need to identify their own sins and address their own failures that they can impose this task on others who are not at that level of maturity. I know I have done this in my ministry. So driven to be more like Jesus, I find it frustrating that others see little need for any deep effort at repentance and contrition. "Don't they know? God seeks to forgive them. If they will only repent, they can have a greater experience of God's wonderful forgiveness!" Or so I insist.

This is in no way meant to judge or condemn. My hope is to liberate and empower each of us to embrace this lifelong journey and surrender to the Spirit's movement in our lives. Let me repeat, the goal is not to achieve. The goal is merely to surrender, to be faithful, and to await the Spirit's good sense of timing and renewal.

8
REGAINING BALANCE

One of the key elements in recovering from burnout and codependence is to regain balance in one's life. During my years directing the Church Renewal Center, the treatment team I gathered there worked with this single goal in mind: to help the clergy who came for our care regain their balance *physically, emotionally, spiritually, and professionally*. In other words, we treated the whole person.

From those years of experience, I have assembled the following strategies to regain balance. Many of these items I have gleaned from Roy Oswald's excellent *Clergy Self-Care: Finding a Balance for Effective Ministry*, but most are my own suggestions.[1] They are grouped under three categories: (1) nurture, (2) advocacy, and (3) wholeness. All of them have merit, but trying to adopt all of them at once may be overwhelming—like trying to eat every dish at a smorgasbord. My suggestion is that you pick no more than two new areas for work in your own life right now. Only after you have mastered those should you return to the list and adopt two more. However you choose to approach it, use this list wisely and with grace.

NURTURE

Practicing good self-care is the most important and effective means of regaining balance or regaining self-control over one's ministry. I refer to this as nurture, for this is the area in which the whole person is truly replenished in many different and soul-satisfying ways.

Continuing Education

We all need time away from the pressures and stress of our ministries. We need time for our own oscillation, to be in the presence of a holy person for edification, inspiration, and renewal. I recommend that every parish clergy have at least twelve days per year set aside for intellectual, spiritual, and practical nurture and at least $1,000 to $2,000 designated in the congregation's budget exclusively for this end. The congregation should insist that the clergy use this time for their own good. Clergy who are not regularly participating in continuing education run the risk of falling behind in learning, awareness, and effective strategies for ministry. Here is a place for clergy to refill their vitality buckets in order to arrive each day with new vim and vigor, new ideas and excitement. Too many clergy do not avail themselves of this kind of opportunity; therefore, for their own good, congregations ought to monitor this actively and assist the pastor in finding and funding the most appropriate opportunities. Keeping the pastor operating at peak performance not only is good resource management but also shows the congregation values sensitive and compassionate relations with the pastor.

Spiritual Direction

The demands of parish ministry are intense and draining. It is easy for our vitality buckets to run dry. We need times of retreat and renewal to replenish ourselves for the tasks at hand. Working with a qualified spiritual director, in my opinion, is essential and as important as continuing education. By "qualified spiritual director," I mean someone who is fully credentialed for that purpose by an accredited institution. In spiritual direction, one's deepest self is opened up to another person; therefore, that person ought to be adequately trained and supervised so that all will be handled safely and beneficially. This is terribly sensitive and important work that must be done with the utmost care and correctness. And again, since the congregation will reap most of the benefit from the pastor's spiritual direction, it is my strong opinion that the congregation ought to pay for the service and ascertain that it is rendered by a competent practitioner.

In my own life, I discovered that one of the greatest benefits of spiritual direction was an increased awareness of God's ongoing presence in my life. Once a month when I would meet with my spiritual director, he would ask me what had happened in my life since we last met, and I would review for him the key events. Then would come the question, "So, what has God been telling you in the midst of all of this?" At first, he would confront me with the same question every month, and each time it would catch me off-guard. I would have to stop and reflect through the chain of events and search for some spiritual thread or flow of grace. Later, anticipating the question ahead of time, I could more easily attune myself to that spiritual thread or flow of grace even as it was happening. It made me more open to the "still small voice" that God often uses. And it enriched my daily life via that openness to God's presence and movement for my sake.

Clergy Support Groups

Gathering regularly with other clergy to share the challenging, frustrating, or perplexing things going on in our congregations is a key to maintaining balance in ministry. When all the right dynamics are in place, such groups are an extremely powerful means of sustenance and renewal. I find that ecumenical support groups are usually best, since clergy of the same denomination are often competitive with one another, which stifles openness: Who has the biggest church or budget? Who is being more successful or creative? We need safe places in a collegial environment guided by a competent leader for the best results; therefore, hiring someone equipped to manage the group is the best way to go. Letting a trained facilitator be the holy person allows everyone else to oscillate and be nourished, supported, and empowered. Denominational judicatory offices often can help groups find trained facilitators.

Therapy

All of us can benefit from some therapeutic conversations with the right clinician from time to time. When things are a mess, we have every right to be upset. We can all be overwhelmed or confused with ourselves, our role, our interactions with family and parishioners. Spending some time with a proper clinician only makes sense. When we get the flu, we go to the doctor; when our emotions and professional lives get out of balance, we ought to go to a qualified professional. Whether it be personal problems like situational or chronic depression or relational problems with a spouse or someone else, there is much in life that is more than we can manage alone. It is the wise and loving person who understands and gives themselves permission to be "off balance" and receive the help they need.

Leisure Time

I strongly recommend that no one work more than fifty hours per week on average. Granted, during holy seasons or times of congregational crisis, there will often be the need for an extralong workweek. But clergy should then not be afraid to claim an extra*short* workweek to make up the difference. It takes time to get away, to "have a life," and refill the vitality bucket. That cannot happen if we are too enmeshed or attached to our ministries. Such an attachment is an addiction and needs to be addressed. It is not healthy for the individual or the congregation.

For instance, at the Church Renewal Center, we found that many clergy do not really have a hobby. Therefore, having a recreation therapist on the staff was crucial. Clergy needed to prioritize time for some fun and play in their lives, and few knew how to do that. Thus time management became another key discipline that the recreation therapist worked on with our clients. This was something most of them had never considered, since they were too busy with their codependence to think of anything else.

Friendships

Establishing our true friendships *outside the congregation* is critical to not becoming enmeshed in our ministries—to having a real, personal support group all our own that has nothing to do with ministry. Here is a place to discuss personal issues that have no business being discussed with members of the congregation, or even other clergy. Remember the theory of oscillation? We are in the congregation to be conduits for God's holiness and not there for our own personal needs. Far too many clergy have members of the congregation as friends, a circumstance that creates confusing dual roles that will ultimately conflict with each other. To maintain healthy boundaries, we can only serve in one role with each person. We are either friend or clergy, and not both! Therefore, find those friendships that are so necessary for healthy emotional care outside the congregation and perhaps even outside of ministry.

Trying to establish our primary friendships within the congregation is a clear illustration of what Gerald May calls an *attachment*.[2] It makes our members a focus of our addiction and all that goes with that. When we are so dependent on that relationship for our *fix*, then it will have a dramatic impact on our practice of ministry. We will lose our professional objectivity. We will find it difficult to invoke any necessary discipline within the congregation because, after all, these are *our friends*. It contaminates the process with personal agendas that cross boundaries and will ultimately be painful.

As clergy, we ought to be *close* to the members of our congregation. That is good and necessary. But there is a critical difference between *closeness* and *intimacy*. The clinical field provides a revealing parallel: therapists need to be close to their clients. That is, they need to establish a solid rapport that makes clients feel safe and secure enough to open up about their deepest concerns. But on the other hand, therapists also must maintain a professional distance to keep the process fruitful and healthy. If a therapist responds to a client by sharing their own deep, dark secrets, the therapist has violated the therapeutic relationship. In the exact same way, clergy need to be close to those in the congregation without becoming intimately attached to them in any sense of the word *intimate*. For our intimate friendships, we need to go outside the congregation.

Let me give an illustration of the negative consequences of not having personal friends and support outside the congregation. I know of a male pastor who retired from his congregation after serving there for many years. He and his wife had become totally enmeshed in the lives of those people. It *was* their life—so much so that when they retired, both of them cried for weeks. So what's wrong with a pastor and spouse so loving the members of their congregation that they would miss them so deeply upon retirement? When there is no difference between being someone's pastor and being someone's personal friend—or even worse, using one's parishioners as one's friends—you clearly have a *dual relationship* with the people you turn to for your personal and emotional support. It complicates the pastor-member relationship, it muddles the holy person dynamics, and it inevitably creates conflict and pain down the road.

Renewed Confidence in One's Calling

None of us got into ministry by accident. It was not some huge misunderstanding. God has called us, and that is important and empowering. God does stand by us, even in the worst of times. By God's grace, we are not alone in this ministry—the Spirit is always with us. And we can have the support and fellowship of our colleagues in the faith. God provides.

The strength of one's conviction is imperative; do what you need to do to sustain it. Attending installation ceremonies or ordination services is something I find helpful and encouraging. Hearing again the words that were once spoken for us can help remind us why we are in ministry and what this vocation is all about. Being reminded that once, hands were laid on our own heads and special prayers were spoken on our behalf renews in us the grace of our vocation. God calls. God empowers. God sustains.

When my oldest child was graduating from high school, he asked me what I would think if he or his sibling wanted to become pastors. I confess, the first thing to come to my head—which, fortunately, I did not say—was, "Are you crazy? You've seen how demanding and draining this life in ministry can be. Why would you want to do that?" My second thought was, "I would be so proud to have one of my children go into the ministry and professional service to our Lord. I think that would be great." But I also did not say that for fear that if they didn't become clergy, they would think they had disappointed Dad and feel guilty. And I didn't want that either.

What I finally did say to my son was, "Son, I would want to know that you are absolutely convinced that you have been called by God into this ministry. Because without the strength of that conviction, you will not survive." And I mean that. We must do all we can to maintain our confidence in God's call.

ADVOCACY

The second category of strategies to regain balance is advocacy or role management. The reason why so many clergy are working seventy or more hours per week is because the work is never done. It is always more than one person can do. Few congregations are adequately staffed; in fact, most are significantly understaffed and do not make up the difference with volunteers. So the load inordinately falls on the clergy, who need to find safe ways to manage it.

Set Annual Goals

Review all the things that ought to be done in the coming year with your congregation's governing board. Prioritize no more than four of those areas for ministry, then write *specific, concrete, measurable, obtainable,* and *time-defined* goals for each of the four areas of ministry. What are the key areas of ministry that need a sharper focus this year? What needs the most attention? Does this require the involvement of a church professional, or can a lay leader take the management role? If it requires a church professional, then what other responsibilities can that person relinquish during this year so that attention can be diverted to this priority area? And who will pick up the slack—or will the slack just be tolerated without judgment?

One example of such a goal might be evangelism and door-to-door outreach. Perhaps the pastor will make a commitment to knock on two hundred doors in the community surrounding the church in the coming year to invite these neighbors to come to your church. That is a decent goal that can be measured and is concrete. The pastor can make quarterly or even monthly progress reports. The governing board can ask, "How is it going? If it is not getting done, then why?" Perhaps there is a good reason, such as the failure to relinquish other responsibilities to create the time needed to go door-to-door. So who will pick up those other responsibilities? And if no one will cover them, can they be left undone? What is working or not working and why? What corrective action is needed midstream? How can we gain success on this goal?

This will also facilitate *evaluation* at the end of the year when it is time to look at how well things went. Was each goal met? Why or why not? What got in the way? What needs to be changed? What part of the organization structure or staffing pattern needs to be adjusted? Often, circumstances beyond the control of the church professional interrupt what is determined to be a priority. When the congregation I served was devastated by an act of arson, we had to abandon our building and work and worship elsewhere. That took the place of all the other priorities at that time, through no fault of the congregation or mine.

If all the goals are properly completed, then adequate reward ought to be forthcoming. This does not guarantee proper compensation, of course, but it makes it easier to justify and harder to deny. And the reward can be more than money; it can be the gift of a special vacation paid for by the congregation or additional vacation days (if additional pay is not available at that time). Congregations with limited assets can be creative in providing such compensation; in whatever form reward comes, it more than pays for itself in the boost in morale it helps provide.

Control Your Own Calendar

If we are working more than fifty hours per week on average; if we have no time for our families; if we have not spent good, quality time with our spouse; if our vitality bucket is bone dry—the fault is totally ours. No one will control our calendars for us; that is entirely up to us. We need to take that responsibility as seriously as anything else we do. It is that important.

When I was a parish pastor, I always took at least one full day and two evenings off each week and as much of Saturday as I could get unless there was a wedding or some other similar event. I found that I needed to mark my calendar long ahead of time or those times would be given away. I would commit to doing something church related on one of my free evenings if, and only if, another evening off was still available that week and I could simply trade. And I made no apologies for not being available on that day off or evening home. I simply said, "I'm booked."

Create a Clear Job Description

What is a reasonable expectation for what the clergyperson is supposed to do in a congregation? If one *well-defined*, *sensible*, and *officially adopted* job description is not on record, then every member of the congregation will have their own set of expectations in mind against which the clergyperson will be measured. It is far better to be measured against one reasonable and fair job description than to try to comply with hundreds of unwritten and often inordinate sets of expectations. Insist on this when you accept a call and review it annually with your governing board.

Set Boundaries

We can and we must set clear and healthy boundaries for ourselves. No one will make us do that, and the congregation will delight in transgressing our boundaries any chance they can get—*if we let them*! Do you know that the word *no* is a complete sentence? For codependents, that is hard to practice; too often, one feels compelled to tag some kind of an explanation onto the *no* in order not to offend anybody: "No, I can't do that because . . ." I will explore boundary issues more thoroughly in chapter 10.

Advocate for Adequate Compensation

A sufficient wage and benefits package is difficult to obtain and maintain in a codependent system that rewards church professionals for being martyrs, victims, heroes, and all the rest. It is nearly impossible to advocate for one's own compensation when such attitudes prevail in the congregation, as it will create tension and disruption. The common and handy belief of most laity is, "Church professionals aren't interested in money. That's why they became church professionals." One layperson went so far as to tell me that if I wanted to make a decent living (not if I wanted to be rich), I never should have become a pastor.

The best time to advocate for fair compensation is when negotiating a new call with a congregation. If they really want to entice you to be their pastor, then you have a bit of the upper hand that you can use in a fair and just way to ensure decent compensation, including vacation time, continuing education time, medical benefits, pension plans, and all the rest. Once you are there, and as the years go by, most congregations find a host of excuses not to pay properly or provide raises. At first sight, receiving no raise or a raise below the cost-of-living increase does not appear to be a cut in *real dollars*. You have the same amount of money as before, but now you are chasing after goods and services that have become more expensive, so in actuality, you just got a cut in "living wages." You can afford less now than before. When that happens, my experience is that someone from the judicatory level needs to call the congregation to account. When dysfunctionality and codependence are in operation, it is hard for church professionals to champion their own cause.

If a congregation really cares about its staff, then at a minimum, cost-of-living increases are a part of doing business. If they cannot afford such raises, then the congregation needs to question its viability or its dedication (usually the latter). And more often than not, the problem is not organizational; the problem is spiritual. The congregation as a whole does not adequately comprehend the commitment and dedication it takes to be the household of God. This is a sure sign of a need to prioritize spiritual growth.

If the inability to pay is a legitimate issue and the pastor wishes to remain in that call, then the honest thing for the congregation to do is to admit that it can no longer claim the full-time services of their pastor, since they are not paying a full-time salary. At first, the pastor may drop back to 90 percent time or whatever is appropriate in direct relation to the salary as measured against a judicatory's recommended salary. Fair is fair.

WHOLENESS

The third category of strategies to regain balance in our lives is wholeness. This is the work we do for our own stress management. Essentially, good stress management is that holistic work we do to benefit body, mind, and spirit—and vocation. It is that regaining balance that has been the theme of this entire chapter, but now on a more personal level.

The balance in life we seek is called *homeostasis*. We get thrown off balance by some stimuli (or stressors) that trigger our arousal mechanism involving the sympathetic nervous system. This is usually called the *fight-or-flight response*. We are biologically wired for this response, and for good reason. It helps us manage a crisis more effectively. Our pulse rate quickens, and blood flows from our extremities to our central organs in anticipation of battle and intense action. Our breathing rate increases. We are ready for whatever may come—that's good.

The problem is that repeated and prolonged stress keeps us in that arousal state and exhausts us. What is supposed to happen once the stressor is gone is that the parasympathetic nervous system kicks in and takes us back to homeostasis, or normal balance. Prolonged stress wears out our bodies, minds, and spirits, and we end up with a dysfunctional parasympathetic nervous system incapable of regaining homeostasis, resulting in negative consequences like physical and emotional diseases as well as spiritual emptiness. Therefore, good stress management is holistic. It involves strengthening our bodies, minds, and spirits to be able to move into arousal quicker and to move out of arousal just as effectively.

Exercise

As noted earlier in the book, an inordinate percentage of parish clergy are overweight. Quite frankly, our bodies are no good to us if we let them go unattended. It is as much a sin to abandon our physical health as it is to abandon our spiritual health. Therefore, it is essential that clergy consult their physicians and work with them to put together an appropriate exercise program.

Nutrition and Addiction Control

Again, neglected bodies are not useful and can actually be a detriment to ministry. So get fit and healthy. Consult your physician or nutritionist and eat properly. Related to this is that clergy need to eschew any addictions such as food, alcohol, mind-altering substances, sex, work, or religion. Remember, religion, used all the wrong ways, can be an attachment that destroys, not empowers and fulfills. Improper religion can be the crutch that cripples.

Relaxation

Many of us have a difficult time giving ourselves permission to do nothing. It seems like such a waste. So even when we are doing ostensibly relaxing activities, such as watching television, we try to multitask with work-related materials so that we still feel productive. We need to learn that it is fine to do nothing every now and then. It doesn't mean we are lazy. In fact, some peace and quiet with some good music and a candle burning with a pleasant aroma might be just the thing one needs. Claim the time and use it well. Meditation can be a key part of "doing nothing." Actually, it is doing something but in a relaxed and calming state that enriches rather than depletes us. For helpful aids to meditation, again I suggest the guidance of a qualified spiritual director.

Spiritual Renewal

This is another critical area that one might think clergy ought to have mastered, but too often, pastors get so busy preparing sermons and Bible studies and all the rest that they seldom take the time for their own spiritual discipline. Even daily prayer is not practiced by all clergy. Daily devotions ought to be a top priority. You can work on this with your spiritual director.

Marital Care

Those of you who are married need to claim time to enrich your marriages and use that time wisely. Plan dates to keep the romance alive. Go for moonlit walks or whatever works for you. You don't have to do things that cost money; just make the commitment of your time. Giving themselves to one another is the most precious thing married couples can do. Dim the lights, light a candle, and just talk to each other—share feelings, wishes, dreams, concerns, passions, and fears. That openness and intimacy is magical, and it works!

At the Church Renewal Center, our most common cases had to do with pastoral sexual misconduct. The vast majority of these clients were married men with devoted wives. Although these wives were there for their husbands, the husbands had gotten so consumed with their ministries and enmeshed in the lives of the members of the congregation that they neglected their marriages and got their needs fulfilled improperly. After becoming heroes and martyrs for the congregation, those who violated their marriage vows did so because they felt *entitled*. They felt they had *earned* that extra attention and affection for having spent so much time away from home and spouse. Enticed by an adoring or needy parishioner, the temptation to accept what they felt they earned proved disastrous.

Family Care

Just as you should claim time with your spouse, claim time for family activities. Maintain proper boundaries between personal and professional time and energy. Both need faithful attention. And again, use the time wisely, as our children grow up way too fast. In a flash, they are adults.

Back in Vermont, our financial resources were quite limited. We scrimped and saved to give our children Friday afternoon gymnastics classes. After the class, we'd all meet to go to Al's French Fries for dinner (yes, I know, nutrition . . .). But it was truly quality family time. We never went to restaurants; we couldn't afford them. But Al's French Fries we could afford. So it was our Friday ritual of blessed family time spent eating and just enjoying each other in the luxury and ambiance of Al's French Fries!

Family-of-Origin Healing

Imperfect parents are a reality we all share, and the need to address issues from our families of origin is a critical piece of wholeness and well-being. We ignore it at our own peril, and we jeopardize our ministries and our relationships with the members of our congregation likewise. We need to come to terms with those hurts, disappointments, inadvertent comments, or whatever our imperfect parents inflicted upon us. Do the therapy to get beyond that or it will contaminate your parenting and your ministry and all your other relationships.

* * *

You are not perfect, and you never will be! But that's no excuse for accepting the imperfections without some effort to address them. Do it for yourself—prove how well you can practice self-care. Do it for our Lord who loves you so dearly. And do it to enrich your ministry.

An empty vitality bucket ends up as a negative influence on the total ministry of your congregation. Do it for your marriage, your children, your extended family, for all those whom you love and who love you. It is the best gift you will ever give them—yourself, happy and contented, enriched and empowered, full of God's love and grace.

A BALANCED LIFE CHECKLIST

Nurture
- [ ] continuing education
- [ ] spiritual direction
- [ ] clergy support group (preferably ecumenical)
- [ ] therapy (if appropriate)
- [ ] leisure time
- [ ] renewed confidence in one's calling
- [ ] friendships outside the parish

Advocacy
- [ ] annual goals (no more than four)
- [ ] control of one's own calendar
- [ ] clear job/ministry description
- [ ] proper boundaries
- [ ] adequate compensation

Wholeness
- [ ] exercise
- [ ] nutrition
- [ ] no addictions (sex, work, food, substances, religion)
- [ ] relaxation
- [ ] spiritual renewal
- [ ] sleep
- [ ] time to sustain/enrich the marriage
- [ ] time to sustain/enrich family life
- [ ] family-of-origin healing

9

STRETCHING AND BRIDGING

In working with the Myers-Briggs Type Indicator (MBTI), one thing we learn is that we cannot hide behind our personality type. That is, just because we have a certain temperament that has a clear propensity to codependence, this does not excuse us from responsibility for our personal behavior. One cannot claim, "It's not my fault. That's just the way I am." Sorry—no excuses allowed. Just because one has certain feelings does not give one license to act at will. For instance, if I act angrily, it is because I choose to be angry. Even though circumstances might provoke such a response, as a freethinking human being, I have the choice to respond with anger or not.

While I strongly believe and ardently assert that it is impossible to have a wrong feeling, I am equally convinced that it is not our emotions that get us into trouble; it is our behavior. Okay, so I feel angry. Now I need to engage my brain and decide what I want to do with that anger. As stated before, from quadrant IV, I can take my anger to quadrant II and seek to dominate and control. I can retreat to quadrant III by taking my anger and directing it back at myself and thereby get depressed. Or I can identify the source of my anger and determine if it is legitimate. If so, I can find some constructive avenue to express my emotion, such as engaging in rational and productive problem-solving so that the cause of my anger can be permanently eliminated and the problem will not recur. I have choices. Just because one is an NF and a natural candidate for being a martyr/victim, prone to rushing in to rescue the members of one's congregation in heroic fashion and volunteering to be the scapegoat for all the discomfort, does not mean one *has* to act in such a fashion.

STRETCHING

In working with personality types, we talk about two primary strategies to compensate for the propensities of our personality preferences: *stretching* and *bridging*. To stretch means to work to adopt the skills and abilities of other personality types. From the beginning, just because one is an ENFP (Extravert, Intuitive, Feeling, Perceiving) does not mean that one lacks ISTJ (Introvert, Sensing, Thinking, Judging) skills or abilities. It merely means that one *prefers* to act in an ENFP fashion. Personality types measure preferences, not abilities.

Therefore, when one's preferences cause a problem, a person can *stretch* and use an opposite function to find a way out. For example, as an Intuitive–Feeler (NF), I can raise guilt to an art form. I am a master at feeling guilty; it comes to me in a flash. I don't have to go looking for it, it's just quickly and naturally there. This guilt has a lot to do with the hypersensitivity of an NF, the natural emphasis on emotions and relationships that is this type's strength and weakness. I am easily entrapped, enmeshed in a situation with someone, attempting to rush in and rescue that person from their pain or discomfort like the family hero I have programmed myself to be. Actually, rescuing and acting like a hero can bring me lots of pats on the back. The problem is that it also gets me entangled in dual relationships and eventually exhausted, frustrated, and disappointed in the outcome.

But I have a choice. When the situation begins to take form, I can stretch to my thinking function. While I prefer to use my feeling function to make decisions, I can embrace some new behavior, stretch my normal course of action, engage my thinking function, and respond to the situation in a more rational way that will keep me from the entanglements of rescuing and all the rest.

Here is a classic example: As a strong NF, I am a hugger. I love to give and receive hugs. When doing pastoral counseling, ending the session with an affirming hug is the natural thing for me to do. But it isn't always the *right* thing to do with every person. For some, it can be appropriate, but for others, it can be intrusive and overwhelming. I need to think about each situation and respond reasonably, not emotionally, to protect my counselee and myself from harm.

Stretching is not easy. It takes concentration. If you are a right-hander, it's like trying to write your signature with your left hand. At first it is awkward; you may feel embarrassed at your ineptness. You need to focus and be far more attentive to the details of writing. But the more one practices using the thinking function, just as one might practice writing with the opposite hand, one can master the ability and find it exceedingly helpful in many ways.

By learning to stretch their abilities and adopt a stronger preference for the thinking function—not in place of good feeling sensitivities but as a balance for those feelings—NFs will find that they function in a more *balanced* fashion that is ultimately more effective.

Intuitive–Thinkers (NTs), who naturally engage their thinking function in lieu of their feeling function, can stretch to their feeling function to seek that balance so desired. NTs are gifted at being enablers and a different kind of family hero (such as always having the answers). They do that from a rational perspective that often fails to take into account all the emotional and relational dynamics involved. Stretching to the feeling function allows them to deal with situations with more sensitivity and to relinquish control.

In the same way, people with Sensing–Judging (SJ) temperaments also serve willingly as chief enablers, coming from a "let's get it right, follow the rules, and maintain tradition" perspective. All that can be very helpful unless what is needed is to go beyond the rules, think outside the box, and be more spontaneous or creative. Then SJs need to stretch to the perceiving attitude that is more flexible, open-ended, and easygoing.

BRIDGING

To *bridge* means to find a colleague or key congregation member who has the personality preferences you lack and to recruit that person to help you see what you do not see, understand in ways you fail to understand, and identify options for action that you may not be able to identify. For example, here I am in my good NF fashion, sensitive and creative, idealistic and eager to make everyone happy. I'll do whatever it takes to ensure there is no conflict and everyone is getting along. That's my style. But I can get things really messed up by stepping on traditions, crossing lines of responsibility, and failing to follow chains of command when I try so hard to keep everyone happy. Therefore, if I bridge to an SJ who knows policy and procedures, rules and regulations, traditions and chain of command exceedingly well, it will save me a pack of trouble. The SJ will help keep me in line, give me solid advice, and avoid the pitfalls of my personality preference.

For an NT, the bridge can be to a Sensing–Feeling (SF) type. NTs are gifted at idealistic thinking that may be out of touch with the realities and the emotions of those involved. SFs will be in touch with the realities and aware of the emotions and can steer the NT to the right course.

The SJ can bridge to an Intuitive–Perceiving (NP) type. SJs are so involved with the concrete, the practical, the traditional—rules and regulations, policies and procedures—that they fail to be open to creative alternatives and flexible solutions. They can fall into the trap of rigidity. An NP will help them open that trap and begin to see alternatives, such as new visions and options, that can be very productive.

Stretching and *bridging* are important aspects of dealing with the limitations of our personality types. I firmly believe that one's strengths, when taken too far, become one's weaknesses. So while my outgoing, creative, sensitive, and flexible nature serves me well in many ways, stretching and bridging into other personality preferences will definitely help me avoid problems and find far better solutions to the natural situations that arise when doing ministry.

No one is complete unto themselves. We all can use some help now and then. To be mature is to accept that outside help—indeed, even to seek it and engage in the dialogue in open and enlightened ways. That's the path to a well-balanced approach that will always work better than even the best we can do on our own.

10

KNOWING
THE BOUNDARIES

I have done presentations on professional boundaries for well over five thousand church professionals from a wide variety of denominations all over this nation, and I am continually amazed at how poorly these people really understand such serious matters. We need to understand that the practice of ministry is not only a calling but also a profession. As with any profession, ministry has its standards of practices, its ethics, its limitations for the sake of the "client" and the "practitioner." I am convinced that the vast majority of clergy are unprepared to understand and maintain the boundaries of our profession.

Perhaps this shouldn't be too surprising. Those boundary-training presentations have included numerous seminary faculty who are often amazed at the proper limits they should be teaching and maintaining themselves. No wonder their students are not better prepared! At one seminary where I did this training, a faculty member informed me that he was having an affair (not including intercourse) with a seminarian, and he wanted my guidance and advice. Talk about trying to "lock the barn after the horse has escaped"! We simply expect more from our faculty members—and that may be our mistake. They are as human as the rest of us.

A HOLY OFFICE

We need to remember that while the theory of oscillation identifies clergy as holy people, that is not so much an ontological statement as it is a functional statement: clergy serve in the *holy office* of ministry. It is the *office* that is holy, not the person.

So while the occupants of this holy office are mere mortals with feet of clay, with faults and shortcomings like everyone else, the duties of this holy office mandate that we function at a higher level than other "mere mortals." This is neither automatic nor easy. It is a huge challenge for mere mortals to live up to the expectations and demands of a holy office. Being human is an excuse clergy often attempt to use when they are not keeping appropriate professional boundaries, but it is a bogus excuse. If we are not prepared to work and live under the elevated standards of a holy office, then we should not occupy that office.

Does this mean we need to be perfect? No. But we do need to be *professional!* After all, the opposite of *professional* is *amateur*. If we fail to meet the proper standard of professional boundaries, then our practice of ministry is amateur. Ministry is too important an office, too critical a service in this post-Christian era, to be done in an amateur fashion. We all should hold this holy office in too high a regard to allow it to sink to an amateur practice.

Yet without exception, when I present this topic before clergy, someone always protests that I am "ruining" the practice of ministry with my professional standards and expectations. Many clergy don't want to be professional. Far too many have in fact entered the office to get their own needs met, to gain a high degree of recognition (quadrant II) or affection (quadrant IV). Some clergy seek to use the holy office as a means to exercise their dominance (quadrant II), while others use it as a means to acquire friends and relationships (quadrant IV) within the bounds of the clergy-to-member interaction. Maintaining good professional boundaries gets in the way and compromises a mode of ministry that they want to practice.

DO NO HARM

One rule needs to be standard for all in the helping professions: "Above all, *do no harm*." When we violate the professional boundaries of ministry, we run a significant risk that harm can be done to our parishioners, to the congregation, to our families, and to ourselves. Violating boundaries breaks the *trust* relationship that is essential for the proper practice of ministry. If people cannot trust their clergyperson (whom they regard as having been *sent to them from God*), then whom can they trust? And if the one sent by God proves not to be trustworthy, then is God trustworthy? Obviously, there is a great deal at stake in keeping professional boundaries.

This is particularly true in regard to sexual boundaries. Violating such boundaries, which are so intimate in nature, stands out from any other transgression in its sensitivity and egregiousness. Yet despite all the horrifying news headlines about such violations in recent years, mixed messages still abound in the church about the proper exercise of sexuality in the parish. On the one hand, we hear more and more about sexual harassment and expensive lawsuits about abuse. In a growing number of states, sexual misconduct can be a felony with serious criminal consequences such as substantial fines and prison time. On the other hand, numerous stories abound regarding church professionals who divorce their spouses and shortly thereafter marry a secretary, parishioner, intern, or someone else with whom they have had a professional relationship. While eyebrows may be raised, too often no other consequences result, which sends the message that as long as you are discreet, it is okay.

Even some seemingly innocuous behaviors, such as hugging, can ride a fine line of appropriateness. For many clergy, including myself, hugging is a sign of warmth and caring. It is thought to be a means of expressing a measure of compassion and connectedness or a physical form of affirmation. The problem is that the *interpretation* of the hug as appropriate or inappropriate, welcomed or intrusive, is not up to the one who *gives* the hug but is the domain of the one who *receives* the hug. So what the clergyperson has in mind in giving a hug doesn't matter;

the interpretation is totally for the one receiving the hug to determine. Therefore, hugging and other such physical expressions—while often a good thing—need to be done with sensitivity and *permission* from the one who is to receive that attention.

In an effort to dispel the mixed messages, and as yet another step in overcoming the effects of burnout and codependence, I write this chapter on boundaries to help guide your decision-making in these sensitive areas. It is neither all-encompassing nor meant as a legal reference. It is not intended to tell you what to do in every instance. My intent is to make a clear and practical presentation of common professional boundaries so that everyone knows when they may be crossing the line. Clergy need to use their own ministerial instincts to discern what to do when and to make wise pastoral choices.

DEFINITIONS AND SPECIFIC ISSUES

In 1992, the Federation of State Medical Boards of the United States gave the following instructions regarding physicians' contact with patients:

> Do not engage in behavior which could be interpreted as sexual or unprofessional. Examples include: sitting too close to the patient; "making eyes at" or giving seductive looks at the patient; inviting the patient to lunch, dinner or social functions; telling sexual jokes or stories; "kidding" in a sexual manner; paying too-lavish compliments or otherwise drawing attention to the patient's appearance; using offensive language; discussing your personal love life; giving or accepting expensive or significant or intimate gifts; touching (either directly on the skin or through the clothing), or using or offering alcohol or drugs.[1]

Such standards apply to all helping professionals, not just physicians. From this description, we can derive three basic principles:

1. "Sexual misconduct usually begins with relatively minor boundary violations . . . [showing] increasing intrusion into the

[parishioner's] space." It can, but does not always, culminate in sexual contact.

2. "Not all boundary crossings or even boundary violations lead to or represent evidence of sexual misconduct."

3. However, "fact finders . . . [e.g., judicatory officials and attorneys] often believe that the presence of boundary violations (or even crossings) is presumptive evidence of, or corroborates allegations of, sexual misconduct."[2]

From this, we can develop these key definitions of what we are talking about:

- A *boundary crossing* is behavior that intrudes upon another person's physical and emotional limitation which that person defines as safe and/or appropriate.
- A *boundary violation* represents a harmful crossing, a transgression of a boundary.
- It is the *victim* who decides if a crossing is harmful or nonharmful.
- *Closeness* is when two individuals' boundaries are in near proximity without either person's boundaries being crossed or violated.
- *Intimacy* is the intertwining of personal boundaries between two individuals *of equal power* (note the theory of oscillation and the *holy person* status). This should always be a mutually agreed-upon situation. Clergy *always* have a higher level of power over every member of the congregation.
- *Confidentiality* requires keeping secret all information regardless of how insignificant and regardless of what motive might be claimed for breaking confidentiality (e.g., "In order to be helpful . . .").

Confidentiality

Strict confidentiality is obviously the norm for clergy communication. Assume confidentiality unless otherwise clearly defined. Written releases are the safest way. (However, disclosure is required in the case of child abuse and suicidal or homicidal intent.)

As church people, we tend to violate one another's confidentiality all the time. Here's a hypothetical example: Let's assume that Mabel, a member of your congregation, is in the hospital, and the congregation has been praying for her. During the Sunday announcements, you say, "I stopped by Mabel's room on the way to church today, and I'm pleased to report she is doing fine. Our prayers have been answered." You have just violated Mabel's confidentiality! Did Mabel authorize you to release that information (no matter how "harmless") to anyone else? How do you know? *Before* leaving the hospital room, you should have asked Mabel's permission to share her good news with the people at church. Just one question, and you would have protected Mabel's confidentiality. It takes less than ten seconds! To violate Mabel's confidentiality, for any reason, no matter how noble, is to violate Mabel.

Remember the rule: do no harm. This is something that is not usually taught and too often taken for granted. In fact, I find that judicatory executives break these confidentiality boundaries as much as anybody. How can the clergy know what to do when those "over them" are violating confidentiality? This business of confidentiality is serious, yet it is treated with little regard. It is *wrong* because our parishioners have the *right* to privacy. To violate a person's privacy, especially as someone who represents God and who ought to be trustworthy, is to violate that person and render the trusting relationship broken and void.

Role Considerations

What is our role as the holy person? We must constantly be asking ourselves, "Is this part of my role as a church professional?" After all, not all requests by members of our congregation are healthy or appropriate. It is the church professional who is responsible for knowing the difference. If someone asks me to do something I am not sure is appropriate, I can politely excuse myself from doing that, stating, "I'm not sure that's the right thing to do at this time, and I don't want to do anything that may cause you harm. I care enough for you not to do that right now."

Avoid falling into a role that fosters *parental dependency*. Remember the clergyperson who carried the elderly lady up the steps to her bedroom every night? That may not have had any sexual connotation, but it sure fostered a parental dependency. But what about the extradependence discussed in the theory of oscillation? That is only temporary. It is for the clear purpose of inspiring, equipping, motivating, supporting, and enabling our congregation members to return to the real world, pick up their intradependence, and change the world. If we keep the members of our congregation stuck in that extradependence, then we are fostering a pathological parental dependency.

Avoid falling into any *dual relationships* such as business partnerships, therapeutic professional relationships, and even close friendships. One cannot be both therapist and pastor. One cannot be both close friend and pastor. As noted in chapter 8, being one's clergyperson and then trying to be one's close friend can cause conflict, drain energy, and even be destructive to both parties. Dual relationships will conflict with each other in a variety of ways; avoid them.

For single pastors, dating a parishioner is *always* a serious dual relationship and boundary violation: "once a parishioner, always a parishioner." An imbalance exists that does not give the parishioner, or even a former parishioner, equal power in the relationship. The church professional always has greater power. Single pastors who wish to date need to find relationships outside their congregational circles.

Time Spent with Parishioners

Make appointments only at proper times: when others are in the building, not at the end of the day when you are there alone. Even the slightest suggestion of impropriety can be damaging to church professional and church member alike. Put time limits on contacts of any kind, including phone calls. If we are paying "too much attention" to one person, that person may assume a more intimate connection than we intend. In the same way, limit the duration of counseling services

provided to a congregational member—no more than three sessions
for nonemergency situations. After that, refer the member to an appropriate therapist. In an emergency situation, have your contacts and
procedures in place so that you know what to do. Know which psychia-
trist to call to get someone admitted immediately to appropriate care.

Place and Space

Counseling and other contacts should be made in an appropriate room
like an office, with a secretary or other personnel nearby. If the congregation has insufficient resources to have those other personnel available, then a system needs to be created to make it safe for everyone.
Carefully recruit volunteers just to be in the building so that you are
not there alone. Explain to everyone ahead of time the purpose of these
volunteers and train them accordingly, particularly regarding confidentiality issues.

Home visits demand careful attention. In all cases, the church professional is the one who must maintain the proper boundaries. Taking
someone along, such as a competent lay leader or professional associ-
ate, is advisable if there aren't other adult family members who can
be present. Lunch or dinner visits can be problematic also. Choose a
public, well-lighted setting. Treat this situation as a clear "business"
function with professional standards. Again, in all pastor-to-member
interactions, the church professional is responsible for even the appearance of impropriety. Conversations in cars can pose similar difficulty;
make other arrangements.

Review of Giving Patterns

I believe that for the church professional to review the financial giving
records of any or all the members of the congregation is a boundary
issue. Such knowledge will potentially bias the clergy, and they will no
longer be "clean" in their relationships. How can we not be affected?
If one family makes little money but is quite generous while another
family makes a lot of money but is quite sparse in their giving, will this

in no way affect our relationships with those families? I don't think so—especially when our salaries come from that giving! The dangers of treating people preferentially or with resentment based on their giving are great. My recommendation is to stay as "clean" as possible and not review financial records unless explicitly necessary. I recognize that many readers will debate this point and that the stewardship people will likely disagree with me. At the very least, clergy need to establish clear guidelines with their governing boards regarding such issues so that everyone in the parish knows and understands these boundaries and can work together with confidence.

Money and Gifts

Giving or receiving gifts can be troublesome; it may symbolize more than the church professional intends. Beware of giving or receiving expensive gifts, personal items, or inheritances and of serving as the executor of an estate. And remember, asking for a favor is asking for a gift, and it may imply an unintended personal involvement. In the same way, providing personal money (even a loan) to a member of the congregation can be problematic. Keep the relationship clearly professional. I suggest that each church professional monitor this activity with regard to the accepted norms for each denomination, region, and local congregation and encourage each congregation to have a clear written policy on this matter. In some congregations, gifts to the clergy at special holidays are common. It is one way the members of the church show their gratitude. If that is the custom, it may be okay, but to *ask* for such gifts is problematic.

Clothing

Keep an appropriate appearance suitable to the occasion or activity. One's appearance isn't how the church professional sees themselves but how others might interpret them. For example, sexually provocative clothing for either gender is inappropriate. Dress to reflect the role of a holy person, keeping in mind the accepted norms for your community and denomination; a proper standard needs to be determined and maintained. Granted, this can be hard to predict—a clergy collar can be a "turn-on" for some!—so it is worth asking appropriate people in the parish and judicatory what the local standards and expectations are regarding pastoral garb.

Language

Be careful about creating a false sense of intimacy. The church professional may know what they mean by a certain expression, but the church member may not. For instance, word choices can violate. It isn't what you *meant* to say; it's how the church member *interprets* what you say. The church professional, who makes a living with words, is responsible for choosing those words wisely. Content, tone of voice, and body language can create an inappropriate atmosphere of affection.

Self-disclosure is a complex issue. To witness and share is one thing; personal testimonials can be a powerful pastoral tool, but to expose oneself verbally is another. Too much openness may imply an improper level of intimacy. How will the church member interpret what you share? Is the self-disclosure appropriate to the context and in service to the ministry? Whose need is being met?

In the same way, the professional's use of their first name may signal an intimacy and familiarity that is not appropriate. The church professional to church member roles need to remain clear. For instance, for me, going by just "Fred" would be problematic in the context of the congregation. Instead, I would have parishioners use "Pastor Lehr," "Reverend Lehr," or just "Pastor" or "Reverend" (if I was Catholic or Anglican, I would have used "Father Lehr" or just "Father"). At the most, "Pastor Fred," "Reverend Fred," or "Father Fred" would be appropriate. Keep the title that clearly defines the relationship.

Physical Contact

A handshake is the safest form of physical contact, but even that can be abused. As already discussed, hugging can be problematic. How does the member of the congregation interpret the hug? Does that person have any kind of abusive situation in their background that might affect how they receive or interpret the hug? Even if initiated by the church member, the control over any physical contact is the responsibility of the church professional. Simply stating "This is not okay" may be best.

SUMMARY

In all cases, the church professional is the person responsible for ascertaining and maintaining proper boundaries. In every case of boundary crossing or violations, regardless of who initiated what, the church professional is the perpetrator and the parishioner is the victim. Determining what is harmful or not is the judgment call of the church member.

Boundary crossings or violations reflect codependent issues and are most likely to happen when the professional is feeling "burned out." Therefore, when they occur, the clergyperson must always ask these questions: Why was I not able to keep a healthy and appropriate professional boundary? What was going on? Where was the impulse control? What need was being met? Was it an issue of controlling others? Was it an issue of being controlled and trying to please others? Was I being a hero, a martyr/victim, a rescuer?

Intimacy in ministry is inappropriate. Closeness in ministry is commended and to be managed carefully by the church professional. At any time, even with your best-planned actions, if any doubt remains or if there is not clarity in general or in a specific instance, get an appropriate, competent, professional consultation from a mental health professional, crisis center, or certified pastoral counselor. This kind of consultation is most helpful when detailed notes of the incident are used. Also, being part of a collegial support group for all professional concerns is recommended.

BOUNDARIES CHECKLIST

The purpose of the following checklist is to encourage discussion and to point out how difficult many of our boundary decisions can be, especially in a system that often rewards codependent, counterproductive behaviors. The checklist is not meant to be a judgmental exercise to emphasize one's failures; rather, it is intended to raise the consciousness of church professionals with regard to keeping healthy professional boundaries. In this litigious society, risk management has become very important. But more than that, church professionals need help to overcome the pressures toward codependence, to practice good role clarity, and to maintain healthy boundaries that will make their ministries more effective, safe, and satisfying.

Boundaries Checklist

1. Should a church professional avoid saying no when church members ask . . .
    for help?   Y   N
    for a favor?   Y   N
    to be rescued?   Y   N

2. Is it appropriate for a church professional to feel like a parent (fostering dependence) to a church member?   Y   N

3. May one be both pastor and friend to a church member?   Y   N

4. Is it permissible to be both pastor and "therapist" to a church member?   Y   N

5. Is it appropriate to be in a business relationship with a church member?   Y   N

6. If single, may a church professional date a single church member?   Y   N

7. If single, may a church professional date a *former* single church member?   Y   N

8. If single, may a church professional date a single counselee?   Y   N

9. If single, may a church professional date a *former* single counselee?   Y   N

10. There is no apparent risk for church professionals to counsel opposite-gender church members alone, with no other personnel in the building.   Y   N

11. How much time a church professional spends alone with a church member is not important.   Y   N

12. Long-term counseling relationships between church professionals and church members/counselees are appropriate.   Y   N

13. Church professionals may visit opposite-gender church members at the member's home with no apparent risk.   Y   N

14. Lunch or dinner meetings with a church professional and an opposite-gender church member are not problematic.   Y   N

15. There is not a problem with a church professional making a personal loan to a church member.   Y   N

16. Having long conversations in a car between a church professional and a church member is without risk.   Y   N

17. A review of the financial giving records of church members by a church professional is not problematic.   Y   N

18. It is not problematic to receive a gift from a church member
    when it is . . .

      an expensive gift.   Y   N

      a personal/intimate gift.   Y   N

19. To receive a gift from a counselee is not problematic.   Y   N

20. Church professionals may be as stylish or casual in their dress as
    they like.   Y   N

21. Suggestive clothing (e.g., short skirts, tight-fitting garments) being
    worn by a church professional is their own business.   Y   N

22. Church professionals are allowed to use any kind of language they
    want.   Y   N

23. Church professionals are allowed to tell off-color jokes/stories to
    anyone, including church members.   Y   N

24. Church professionals are allowed to drink alcoholic beverages
    with church members.   Y   N

25. When alcoholic beverages are served at a wedding reception or
    similar event, the amount that a church professional consumes is
    not problematic.   Y   N

26. If church members are sensitive about certain topics of conver-
    sation, that is their problem and of no concern to the church
    professional.   Y   N

27. Sharing information about oneself and one's family as a church
    professional to a member/counselee is appropriate.   Y   N

28. To be called by only their first name by church members is not
    problematic for a church professional.   Y   N

29. Is the church professional free to break confidentiality when sincerely attempting to help a church member/counselee?   Y   N
     Just with a close friend?   Y   N
     Just with a family member?   Y   N
     Just with another professional?   Y   N

30. It is not necessary to get written permission from the counselee to get a consultation regarding counseling from another professional.   Y   N

31. Church professionals may hold hands with a church member/counselee during counseling.   Y   N
     May hug a member/counselee   Y   N
     May kiss a member/counselee   Y   N
     May sit next to a member/counselee on a couch   Y   N
     May meet in a dimly lit room with a member/counselee   Y   N

32. If a church member/counselee initiates/requests a hug, kiss, hand holding, and so on from a church professional, then there is not a problem.   Y   N

33. How the words and actions of a church professional are interpreted and perceived by a church member/counselee is not the responsibility of the church professional.   Y   N

34. It is the church professional who determines if a word or action is a boundary violation.   Y   N

35. Ministry and intimacy go together; it is unavoidable.   Y   N

36. Much of this boundary stuff is just an overreaction to isolated incidents and doesn't really apply to me.   Y   N

* * *

From a risk-management perspective as well as a role-clarity perspective, the preferred answer to every item is *no*. I want to protect church professionals from litigation. But even more, I want to assist church professionals to have clear, clean, and healthy relationships with all their church members and counselees. All will benefit from the observance of proper professional boundaries.

11
BECOMING EMPOWERED

But he said to me, "My grace is sufficient for you, for power is made perfect in weakness."

—2 Corinthians 12:9

Only when we center ourselves in the gospel, develop our spiritual maturity, regain balance in our lives, and learn to maintain proper boundaries can we hope to overcome the effects of burnout and codependence. Now we are ready to seriously consider our power and how one uses it or loses it.

POWER CURRENCIES

What is *power*? I define it as "the ability to get what I want." Powerful people get things their way. That's how we know they are powerful: they are able to manage the outcome in their favor. What makes people so powerful? They have what are called *power currencies*—the pennies, nickels, dimes, dollars, tens, and millions of power. Some things have very little power; others have a lot of power. For example, power can be derived from education, job title, authority, manipulation, coercion, selfishness, anger/threats, stereotyping, and being stubborn. But power is also derived from kindness, politeness, appreciation, a pleasant appearance, cheerfulness, helpfulness, being accepting, flexibility, and being easygoing. Of course, neither list is exhaustive; one could go on and on.

So if we possess many of these common power currencies (hopefully, the most positive ones), why aren't we all getting what we want all the time? Because of the various ways by which we diminish our power.

First, we choose the *wrong* power currencies. And that needs to be understood in two ways. First, we need to know our context. For example, in order to become a pastor, I needed to complete one semester of clinical pastoral education. I did mine working with juvenile delinquents, where we were taught how to do group therapy with these teenagers. If I went to start a group session by politely saying, "Okay, gang, it's time to start. Let's all sit down and get quiet," they would have said I was lame. But if I yelled at them, "Shut up, sit down, get quiet!" then they would say, "Oh, *the man* means business. We'd better pay attention." This use of power got their attention and respect. However, if I began a meeting of the governing board of my congregation by yelling, "Shut up, sit down, get quiet!" I don't think it would go over as well. They would be rightfully offended.

Second, we can divide all power currencies into two groups: *long-term* power currencies and *short-term* power currencies. A long-term power currency is one in which the more I use it the more likely I am to get what I want. In the same way, the more I use a short-term power currency, the less likely I am to get what I want. So for instance, what sort of a power currency is my education? Who cares that I have a doctorate? The more I rub that degree in someone's face, the less likely I am to get what I want. As a rule, respect is earned, not demanded. The same with job title and authority: the more I throw my weight around as a department head and demand that people bow to my wishes, the more they will be disgusted and rebel.

Manipulation? A person can probably manipulate you once, maybe twice. But the third time that person tries to manipulate you, you are likely going to be prepared, and it isn't going to work. The same goes for coercion, selfishness, anger/threats, stereotyping (us vs. them), and being stubborn. Those are all short-term power currencies. Many others are all too commonly used in congregations—gossip, parking lot conversations, misused financial giving, the keeping of tradition, cliques, general complaining, coalitions, and the like. They all can work well for a while, but sooner or later, people get tired of them, and they just don't work anymore.

But look at my other list: kindness, politeness, appreciation, a pleasant appearance, cheerfulness, and being considerate, accepting, and easygoing. As a rule, we never get tired of people who have these qualities. In one human relations lab I attended with about forty top-notch professionals, many of whom were therapists or other behavioral science people, we were asked to evaluate who were the most powerful among us, who were most likely to get what they wanted. Early on, the group identified one particular woman as particularly powerful, and her power only grew as the lab continued. She was not dominating or overpowering. She was a gentle soul, soft-spoken, who went to every-one at the lab and asked why we were there and what she could do to help us get what we wanted from the week. She did this with sincerity and integrity. It was her nature to be thoughtful and caring, and that came through easily. So people resonated with her and were willing to go along with her, trusting that she would do us no harm.

There is *power made perfect in weakness*. The same sort of power could be seen in Mother Teresa: she was not a threatening presence but a person whose love of God and people came through and enticed others to go along with her holy "madness" that touched the lives of so many in such a tender way. Or consider Mohandas K. Gandhi, a diminutive man whose physical presence would terrify no one. Yet through nonviolence and active resistance, this unimposing man lib-erated a whole nation from tyranny and oppression. In both of these people, we see power made known in weakness.

CHOOSING OUR POWER CURRENCIES

So what power currencies are we choosing? Long-term ones that will work more effectively the more we use them? Or short-term ones that work less and less the more we use them? Another reason we dimin-ish our power is that we squander it by pursuing the wrong goals.

Go back to my definition of *power* and insert one word: "power is the ability to get what I *really* want." That's the key.

In my own life, even though it took me forty years, I finally discovered what I really want out of life. First, I want an ever-growing relationship with God that brings me closer and closer to the holy. I want to mature in that faith and be blessed with more moments of life in the Spirit. I want a deep sense of satisfaction and contentment with life, a peace that "surpasses all understanding" (Phil 4:7). I want a release from trying to prove something or achieve something and learn to be content with who I am. I want to invest my days in truly meaningful endeavors that make this a better world. I want to love my wife, my children, and my grandchildren openly and unashamedly. I want to be so in tune with my Lord that fear just melts away—even the fear of death. And I am convinced that if I can have that ever-closer relationship with God, then all my other relationships will be better too. I will be a better husband, father, and grandfather. Life will come together in more enriching ways.

Second, I want genuinely to *like* the person I see when I look in the mirror. I want a self-esteem that brings tranquility to my heart and mind. I want to know that I am the best me I can be, and that is just fine.

Who can deny me those two things? Who can take them from me? The evil one will try. But for evil to succeed, I need to cooperate—which I do all too often. The absolute truth, however, is that the two things I really want for my life are mine, free and clear, for the taking. No mere mortal can deny me. It is only me who gets in the way.

Yet another way we diminish our power is that we give it away. For instance, too often when someone says something offensive or hurtful to us, we react something like this: "Do you know what she said? It was awful. I'm so distraught. I can't eat. I can't sleep. I just can't get over it. That was so cruel and mean. How could she say that? I am so upset . . ." We just gave our power away.

As stated earlier, there is no such thing as a wrong feeling. Our emotions are not what gets us into trouble; what we *do* with them is the problem. Okay, so we have been offended. That's a fact. And we have a right to be upset. That's a fact too. But to be sleep deprived and undernourished just doesn't make sense.

What leaves us so vulnerable is our low self-esteem (quadrants III and IV) or our false sense of esteem that comes out in our dominating (quadrant II). A key word in recovery from codependence is *detach*. Let go. Of course it was hurtful, but don't dwell on it. Such hurtful talk says more about the one who said it than about the one of whom it was said. So what if she said horrible things about you? Are they true? No. So let go. Ignore it. The falsehood is not yours but the other person's. Let *her* stay awake all night!

When you detach, you embrace that close relationship with the holy and affirm the person you see in your mirror. When you detach, you can give yourself a good night's sleep and proper nourishment. Don't ruminate over someone else's codependency; that's their problem. We give our power away when we let those other codependent people get to us.

Viktor Frankl's classic book *Man's Search for Meaning* provides a dynamic example of this principle.[1] Frankl was a Jew who survived the Nazi death camps, which, as we all know, were places of utter despair, totally void of hope. If it was a good day, the detainees would only be abused and tortured. If it was a bad day, it was their turn to die. That's how hopeless things were in the death camps.

Understandably, most of the detainees walked around with their heads down and their shoulders bent, visibly showing their despair. But Frankl noticed that some of the detainees still held their heads high and their backs erect. These few detainees knew the truth. Yes, you can torture and abuse me; that is true. You can even kill me; that is true. *But* it is also true that you cannot take my self-esteem, my self-worth, my dignity—*unless I give it to you.* Even in the Nazi death camps, self-respect could be found.

Self-respect and dignity are gifts from God that no one can take from us *unless we give them away.* But we do give them away far too often. Empowerment means that we no longer give away our self-esteem or our dignity.

Finally, there are those who diminish their power because they never learned what it means to have power. Primarily, I am thinking of individuals raised in terribly dysfunctional families. For instance, in a family where Dad is an alcoholic, the kids often find that Dad gets drunk and beats them regardless of how they behave. How are those kids ever going to learn the meaning of self-esteem or dignity? They're up against nearly impossible odds, so they never learn the meaning of their own power. Those who never learn how to have or use power believe that they are not entitled to get things their way, they are afraid of offending, they don't want to make waves. So they go through life denying themselves needlessly.

EMBRACING EMPOWERMENT

I ardently believe that God endows us with all the power we will ever need. We are just so lousy at using it. We squander our power by pursuing the wrong goals. We choose the wrong power currencies—short-term instead of long-term ones. And we give our power away.

But that does not need to continue. This is the day the Lord has made; it's time to detach, pray, surrender to the movement of the Spirit in our lives, and lovingly affirm the person we see when we look in our mirrors. Nothing can take those things from us—only ourselves. That's power of the ultimate kind. That's God's gift to us. Let's use it as God intends—for our own contentment and for a better world.

12

UNTRASHING THE TEMPLE

Do you not know that your body is a temple of the Holy Spirit within you, which you have from God, and that you are not your own? For you were bought with a price; therefore glorify God in your body.

—1 Corinthians 6:19–20

Codependence and burnout are maladies that strike hard and sap energy and hope; they have a detrimental impact on our ability to function and diminish the strength of the church. They are as much a virus in this "body" as anything else. Codependence, in particular, is a serious and deadly pathology that for too long has been ignored, denied, and undertreated. Empowered by God's grace, we can find the courage to accept the diagnosis so that we can embark on the cure. Without that honest diagnosis, no cure can even begin.

Imagine with me, if you will, that you have been saving your money to make a special trip. It is a pilgrimage you have been promising yourself for a long time. Your journey becomes a reality, and you travel to that extraordinary holy place that you have long wanted to visit.

Upon entering your holy place, you find much that disappoints you. The hallways are littered with the refuse left by previous visitors. The walls and ceilings are thickly draped with spider webs. The great works of art are covered with dust. The air is heavy with a stench of vile odors. And worst of all, obscene graffiti has been scribbled on the walls.

What had promised to be an exciting, inspiring event ends in disgust and bitter disappointment. Why would anyone allow such a sacred place to become so full of trash, to suffer such humiliation and disgrace? Certainly those in charge should know better. They must be held accountable to make amends and to "untrash" this holy premise. It is an intolerable situation.

Such a scenario would collectively and individually raise our ire. Yet there are such holy places suffering a similar disgrace clearly in our view every day. In too many ways, we have trashed the temples we call our bodies. If we smoke, we have filled our passageways with deadly fumes. If we overeat, our poor nutritional habits have littered our blood vessels and tissues with the refuse of such carelessness. If we're sedentary, our lack of proper exercise has burdened our bodies with excessive poundage, detracting from the beauty of God's creation and causing great strain on our hearts. The list of sources for the "trash" can go on.

Emotionally and spiritually, we have not done our best either. Jesus announced that he "came that they may have life, and have it abundantly" (John 10:10b). We can't have that abundant life unless we take better care of ourselves—body, mind, and spirit—totally, not fragmentally.

Certainly, any temple so disgraced as the one in our opening scenario would move us to a bold and active response. So why not take an equally bold and active response to the care and nurture of our own bodily temples that God has claimed by the very sacrifice of Christ on our behalf? To trash our personal temples—body, mind, and spirit—is to disturb and disappoint our Creator and Redeemer.

This need not be the case. We can "untrash" our temples. We can seek better emotional health and care. We can keep our intellect sharp and alert with a steady dose of cerebral stimulation. Too often, we take our own spiritual welfare for granted: we never grow in depth and breadth, we seldom challenge the simplicity of our beliefs, we allow a deadening complacency to grow in our souls. We have impoverished our spirituality with the obscenities of materialism, self-centeredness, fear, and despair.

Body, mind, and spirit: our temple in which the Holy Spirit dwells has been bought for us at an enormous price. It was meant for our enjoyment and as an efficient device whereby we might serve our Lord. But we have ignored it or, even worse, abused it. It is time to "untrash the temple." Each of us can live a new life guided by faith and with the knowledge of good nutrition and good physical, mental, and spiritual health. Saint Paul wrote, "Therefore, do not let sin exercise dominion in your mortal bodies, to make you obey their passions. No longer present your members to sin as instruments of wickedness, but present yourselves to God as those who have been brought from death to life, and present your members to God as instruments of righteousness" (Rom 6:12–13).

It is time to address the codependence that has infiltrated the church with its disease. As the trash noted above should raise our ire, even so does this codependence pain us all. It impairs the clergy. This disease has traveled to us over generations. It has become so genetic, so a part of our culture, so ingrained that it is hard to envision the church without it. But we must—this disease should not be passed on.

It is time to address the problem and take bold steps to get ourselves free from our attachments—our minimizations, denial, and delusions. We can dare to identify in which quadrant of the Codependence Graph we are and thereby develop a treatment regime for ourselves.

It is time to look at our personality types and the propensities that go with them. What are our natural pitfalls? How have we fallen prey to them? And what measures do we need to take to stretch, bridge, and move ahead?

It is time to review the codependent roles and admit which ones we fulfill. How have we enabled, rescued, or served as the family hero? Have we allowed others to scapegoat us? Do we feel like the lost child? When we have the confidence to name our roles and launch an effort to overcome them, we set into motion a process that awakens a new hope within us.

It is time to comprehend our "holy person" dynamics so that we can empower and inspire, challenge and support all who have come to us as conduits of God's holiness. We can serve them better when we understand the whole picture.

It is time to untrash the temples that are our bodies, our lives. It is also time to untrash the church from its disease. The two depend on each other. Clergy and judicatory executives will make true progress toward existing in the quadrant of interdependence only when together we engage both ourselves and the church in this pilgrimage to recovery.

It is time to muster the strength to endure the discomfort and disorientation of embracing a new version of reality. It is time to establish and maintain professional boundaries.

It is time to band together so that we can more successfully swim against the tide of our codependent culture. It is time to establish a counterculture movement centered on our faith and the power of God's love. It is time to address our spiritual maturity or lack thereof, to identify where we are in that process, and to seek the Spirit's blessings of greater maturity.

It is time to break free of all efforts to trap us in triangulation or get us enmeshed. Instead, we can detach and be liberated. It is time to take seriously our duty to show up every day with our vitality buckets at least reasonably full so that we can dispense the energy, hope, and love our people so deeply desire. It is time to understand that codependence is a *shame-based disorder*. Our faith teaches us that we need never feel shame. Shame is an attack on our dignity. Guilt is a confession of misdeeds. There is a critical difference that we need to honor and demonstrate in our own lives.

Because we are the church, there is hope. Because this is God's church, there is hope. Because we dare to have faith in God and put our trust in God, there is hope. Together, let us dedicate ourselves to this holy task. In faith, we can find that road to recovery. Together, the church can find its way to recovery. Together, in God's good grace, there is renewal, there is freedom, there is opportunity, there is the chance for recovery, there is hope—always hope.

13
SURVIVING TURBULENT TIMES

Turbulence. That's the right word for it.

Turbulence—violent disturbance or agitation.

Turbulence—radical upheaval.

That is a great term for our times—especially for people in ministry.

Turbulence, disorder, unrest—these words capture the reality of ministry in this day and age.

I am writing this chapter in the year 2020, when many things are disturbed, agitated, and in upheaval. I intend to address the various elements of this turbulence, then share some words of wisdom to help us all find level and solid ground on which to plant our feet and rest our souls so the work of ministry can continue faithfully.

In recent years, several high-profile pastors have admitted to burnout and depression. One pastor admitted, "I feel so distant from God."[1] Indeed, pastors have found ministry impossible for a range of reasons. Of course, a good number of these are older ministers who simply retire—no surprise. But many are not retirees. One primary issue is financial. As noted in the preface to this revised and expanded edition, a 2016 Duke University study found that clergy compensation had significantly dropped in recent decades.[2]

If a new minister goes straight from college into seminary, the accumulation of academic debt can be sizable. Add the debt from college to the debt from seminary, and the sum is daunting. However, many "first-call positions" do not pay well. A small congregation or even a cluster of small congregations struggles to meet its budget and has very limited resources to compensate the minister. It isn't right. It isn't fair. But it is what it is. And that is a harsh reality. Therefore, the minister is challenged with the dilemma of wanting to be faithful to the calling to serve the church while having to pay off great debt. Add car payments or other such routine obligations for supporting a family, and sustaining a household becomes nearly impossible. How can I serve my Lord if I can't even pay my bills?

Another factor in the decision to leave the pastorate is the overall loss of members in mainline denominations, resulting in many pastors feeling discouraged about the meaning and even the feasibility of their work. A 2019 Pew Research Center study noted, "The data shows a wide gap between older Americans (Baby Boomers and members of the Silent Generation) and Millennials in their levels of religious affiliation and attendance. More than eight-in-ten of the Silent Generation (those born between 1928 and 1945) describe themselves as Christians (84%), as do three-quarters of Baby Boomers (76%). In stark contrast, only half of Millennials (46%) describe themselves as Christians; four-in-ten are religious 'nones,' and one-in-ten Millennials identify with non-Christian faiths."[3]

I recently did a small case study of college students who claimed no religious preference. Assisted by Dr. Gina Finelli of the sociology department at Anne Arundel Community College, I asked these students to talk with me about four ideas:

1. Tell me what having no religious preference means.
2. Tell me about hope.
3. Tell me about trust.
4. Tell me what you think happens when you die.

My key finding was that 100 percent of these students were indifferent when it comes to church. They were neither against the church nor attracted to it; they were just plain uninterested. I also discovered that they were already second- and third-generation unchurched. Church provided no frame of reference for them. It was neither good nor bad;

it was just not in their realm of experience. Please note, their being second- and third-generation unchurched means that their children will be third- and fourth-generation unchurched. The trend only continues, and the number of nones gets larger.

The students identified no universal source of hope that one can always depend on. They named no holy or sacred One in whom we can all confidently place our trust. Hope and trust for them were purely transactional, much like a business agreement, based on the mutual ability of two people to have hope in and to trust each other. Likewise, if I am trustworthy, people will trust me. They stressed that we can't trust everyone; we must be cautious. My observation: this is not a very comforting way to live.

Regarding their belief in what happens when we die, all had either no idea or a sense of something positive. A few believed in some kind of heaven but had no concept of what that meant. Interestingly, none—not one—believed in hell. So to say "Come to Jesus so you don't burn in hell" is just not going to work anymore. (Of course, it was never a good idea anyway.)

With generations progressively unchurched, organized religion is in deep trouble. And congregations will continue to struggle.

A 2019 forecast by the Office of Research and Evaluation of the Evangelical Lutheran Church in America (ELCA) calculated the following projections for the denomination:

Baptized membership

2017: 3,458,839
By 2025: 1,816,735
By 2050: 66,540

Average worship attendance

2017: 899,000
By 2025: 604,601
By 2041: 15,811[4]

Frightening. With numbers diminishing like this, obviously congregational finances will be in a terrible condition. And who will get blamed? The minister. And who suffers the consequences? The minister. So one reason many ministers leave the pastorate is financial—both personal and congregational.

As I write, another huge impact on the church is COVID-19. The pandemic has everything inside out and upside down. Nothing is "normal." Worship and choir rehearsal are not as usual. Pastoral care and visitation are challenged. Christian education, confirmation, and vacation church school cannot happen the way they always did. Weddings and funerals, committee meetings, and all the usual organization and administration efforts have to be carried out in different ways. Turbulence!

With the broad and imposing impact of this novel coronavirus comes the economic reality of massive layoffs in the broader society. Millions of people have lost their jobs, many losing their health insurance as well because it was tied to their employment. This only exacerbates the harsh financial circumstances, both personal and organizational. How ministers and ministries will survive is hard to predict.

The changes are disturbing and upsetting. Turbulence.

And as if that were not enough, cultural shifts are occurring as well. The LGBTQIA+ movement is one such shift. Increasingly, our culture is finally accepting people as they are and not judging them based on whom they love. Yet these new attitudes require a social transformation of some measure—more troublesome for some folks than for others. And it is often the minister who charts the course for the congregation to navigate this change.

Just as we have been coming to terms with issues of sexual orientation, a much-needed, long-overdue revival (or perhaps just awakening) of the antiracism movement arises. While many are saying, "It's about time," not all people agree. Like any social change, the issue has stirred up resistance and brought its own set of challenges to ministry. Black Lives Matter. Native Americans. Asians. Jews. Muslims. We don't want to discriminate. Who is charged with managing all of this social reorientation in the course of ministry? In many cases, the burden rests with the ministers themselves.

Climate change is yet another challenge to be recognized, although some remain who deny its significance or the human role in it. As with all these issues, the adjustments seldom go easily. And frequently, it falls on the shoulders of the minister to make changes happen smoothly and comfortably, without conflict. Good luck!

How do those in ministry survive in the midst of all this turbulence?

I suggest a few "words of wisdom" gathered over my forty-eight years of ordained ministry.

WHAT'S IT ALL ABOUT, ANYWAY?

Stephen Covey is a management guru who has an expression I really like: "The main thing is to keep the main thing the main thing."[5] Makes sense.

So what is the main thing for the church? Surely it is the gospel of Jesus Christ.

What is the gospel of Jesus Christ? I firmly believe it is four things. And it is all four—not just one or two. To faithfully practice the gospel is to do all four. No shortcuts. I discussed this at length in chapter 6, but let me address it briefly again.

First, *gospel* means "good news." To "do" gospel is to be people of the good news, not the bad news. The tomb is empty; Christ is risen! That is fantastic good news!

Second, this good news gives us a hope that cannot die. Because Jesus has conquered death, nothing can stop or inhibit the hope that Jesus uniquely provides.

Third, this risen Lord loves us unconditionally—without and beyond all conditions. Jesus never says, "I will love you if . . ."; Jesus always says, "I love you regardless."

Finally, the good news, hope, and unconditional love empower us to claim an open future. Our future is no longer determined by our past. We are free to be all that God wants us to be. Only our own faults and failures hamper the wide-open promise of the future. Yet God prevails.

To practice gospel involves good news, hope, unconditional love, and an open future. I strongly recommend that we present these life-giving and hope-inspiring truths throughout our ministries boldly and often. I wove them into many of my sermons. I mentioned them in newsletter articles. I rehearsed them over and over for the congregation. The point is to insert these four wonderful truths deeply into the DNA of the ministry, to ensure that every member knows them and knows them well.

That's what it's all about. And with that guiding principle, all the rest falls into place and flows logically. Without that clear and sharp understanding of the one main thing, we get a plethora of "main things" floating about in the ministry, only serving to make things more difficult.

The main thing is to keep the main thing the main thing. Review chapter 6.

TAKE YOURSELF SERIOUSLY, BUT NOT TOO SERIOUSLY

Review chapter 8, "Regaining Balance." If we do not take good care of ourselves, we will be no good to anyone else. And as the turbulence rises and gains force, there is all the more reason to maintain a healthy body, mind, and soul. This effort requires us to embrace a faithful dedication to enhancing relations within the ministry and to keeping them strong and healthy.

We work no more than fifty hours per week on average. We exercise and eat properly. We learn how to let go and just do nothing from time to time. We learn how to meditate.

Yes, we strive to do all these healthy things, but we don't do them too seriously. We are only human, and we have our limits. My faults and failures are enough to keep me humble. So we expect from ourselves only what is reasonable. Work hard, yes. But also play and relax and, please, don't take yourself too seriously.

KNOW YOUR LIMITS

Return to chapter 10 on boundaries. In my experience, more ministers get themselves into hot water by not maintaining healthy boundaries than anything else. We especially need to avoid dual relationships. We cannot be both therapist and minister to the same person. Dual relationships just trip all over themselves.

We also cannot be both best friend and minister to the same person. By "best friend," I mean someone with whom we share our secrets. We cannot be *intimate*, allowing the emotional boundaries of two individuals to intertwine. We can be *close* with those in our ministries, though, allowing emotional boundaries to be in proximity without overlapping. In the latter, a proper emotional—and physical—distance is maintained. We need to know the difference.

BUILD THE FOUNDATION BEFORE YOU BUILD THE HOUSE

One suggestion I highly recommend is to immediately build a source of strength and connectedness—a solid rapport with parishioners and especially lay leaders—in any new ministry. If you haven't done that, make it a priority right away.

When I first entered a congregation, I would visit people in their homes. In a smaller congregation, with average worship attendance of one hundred or fewer, I would visit every household as quickly as possible. In a larger congregation, I would ask the lay leadership to identify the twenty most influential people in the congregation, and I would visit them first.

During these visits, I would carefully and lovingly get to know the people. Who are they? What about their families? What's important to them? What do they most like in the ministry? What do they think needs to change in the ministry? How do they think that change ought to happen? And so on.

I would also introduce myself by sharing a bit of my background and what I'm all about. I would briefly introduce my family and the things we like to do. And then I would begin to build support for the things I thought this ministry needed to address. Establishing that rapport is a critical piece that pays off later when turbulence begins. The connectedness builds a level of trust that can enhance all the work that comes after.

THINK LONG TERM, NOT SHORT TERM

Don't go for the quick fix.

I admit that I am not a patient person. I like to get things done and move on. However, especially when working within a voluntary organization, change normally is difficult enough without turbulence.

To facilitate any adjustments—large or small—that are needed to improve the ministry, plan a slow and steady process. Take small steps that can be accomplished without a great deal of effort or stress. Strive for clear progress, and celebrate the little things along the way. One victory leads to another, so rejoice in each completion. Build momentum.

One congregation I served needed to expand the building as soon as possible. By taking small steps and making gradual interventions over a three-year period, when it came time to make the big decision about the project, I had nearly unanimous support. I heard comments such as "You mean we haven't decided that yet? We've been discussing it forever. Sure, let's do it."

The bigger the decision, the greater its impact. The more support needed, the more patient and precise the process needs to be. Success grows success.

MATCH THE MAGNITUDE OF THE EFFORT
TO THE MAGNITUDE OF THE PROBLEM

Don't spend ten dollars on a one-dollar problem. But also, don't spend one dollar on a ten-dollar problem.

Big problems deserve a big effort. Little problems need only a limited effort. Makes sense. But too often, we fail to accurately understand the magnitude of the problem. Either we minimize and pay too little attention to the difficulty or we exaggerate and pay too much attention. In our eagerness to avoid complaints, we tend to commit too much energy to minor problems, leaving us with too little energy left for the big problems. We need to be aware enough to know the difference.

How big is the issue before us? To what extent do we need to invest our resources to resolve it? We need to get a clear handle on the situation and respond appropriately.

REMEMBER, AN OPINION IS JUST AN OPINION AND NOT A FACT

Too often, we get bent out of shape by someone's opinion of this or that. Please understand that an opinion is just an opinion, not a fact. Everyone is entitled to their own opinions. Everyone is *not* entitled to their own facts. We need to sort that out.

Is the view you've heard the opinion of one person (or a few people) and not a hard-and-fast fact? We get so worried about keeping conflict to a minimum that we tend to react to any opinion that comes along. If it's just an opinion, we can acknowledge it and appreciate it, but it may not call for any action. We can just listen and say "Thank you."

However, the opposite is also true: a fact is a fact and not just an opinion. When the facts are clear and prove accurate, we need to go into action. When a large number of people share the same opinion, we ought to pay attention and check out whether it is substantial enough to be considered a fact.

AVOID BINARY THINKING

When addressing a problem like those we face in these turbulent times, we need to try as much as we can to avoid binary thinking—that is, the notion that the solution is either *this* or *that*.

Binary thinking functions in one part of the brain. When we expand the options to three or more, the processing moves to a different part of the brain, which deals with creativity. Decisions made in a binary fashion are less likely to turn out well than are those made in a more creative manner. Just increasing the list of possible solutions frees us to delve into a problem more comfortably and freely. Of course, we can go too far generating options, which can lead to analysis paralysis. We don't need a *host* of options.

For example, with COVID-19, congregations had to decide whether to gather for worship in the church building. Some addressed the question as a yes-or-no situation: "Yes, we'll go back to worshipping as we always did" or "No, we can't do anything until this whole virus thing is resolved." A better approach would be to say, "Yes, we can do that when . . ." Then leaders could label all the conditions that need to be met to again worship together safely.

Yes-or-no decisions need to be kept to a minimum so we can be open-minded and creative in our decision-making.

STRIVE TO BALANCE IDEALISM AND PRACTICALITY

I confess that I am a huge idealist. You may have guessed. I like to dream of the true and noble possibilities and am upset when we settle for anything less than what is pure and right. Get the picture? That has gotten me into trouble more than once. I can be like a drum major marching four blocks ahead of the band, hoping they will catch up. Not a good idea.

So I have learned to do some "reality testing": Is this realistic? Does it meet the test of being practical? Does it stand a prayer of working?

Idealism is wonderful. We need to dream dreams and dare to fulfill them. But being practical makes good sense too. We need to balance those two opposites and find the middle that will work, not sacrificing the ideals but applying them in a feasible way.

DETERMINE WHETHER YOU REALLY NEED THE MAJORITY'S APPROVAL

In ministry, we tend to believe we can't do anything without the approval of the congregation—we need a congregational vote to go ahead. Really? Very often, this is not so. If an effort doesn't involve the whole ministry, why do we need the whole ministry's consent to go ahead?

If an idea is good, it only takes a few people to make it happen, it doesn't impact the rest of the ministry to any significant degree, and it is in keeping with the goals and mission of the ministry, then once that critical mass is achieved, we can go ahead. Obviously, the "critical mass" depends on the effort being considered; it is contextual.

We worry too much that we will get negative feedback if we don't get congregational approval. We want cover for when the complaints come in. On the other hand, when they do, we can explain that we went ahead with the given endeavor because it was in keeping with our goals, values, and mission, and we had the critical mass we needed to get it done. We didn't need everyone. It didn't involve everyone, so why trouble them with making the decision?

IF YOU'RE GOING TO BE A MARTYR, BE SURE THE ISSUE IS WORTH IT

This principle follows the wisdom that we should spend ten dollars' worth of effort for a ten-dollar problem.

Yes, there are some things—like antiracism—for which we must draw a line and say, "Here I stand!" (I read that somewhere.) If we fail to take those stands when they are evident, when it is a clear violation of the ministry's values and beliefs, we compromise our ministry and our own self-worth. We diminish our integrity and our honor as human beings. We sacrifice our dignity and call into question others' trust in us.

When it is time to stand firm, by all means, we must stand firm.

But we need to be sure the battle is worth fighting and perhaps even losing in the short term as we march toward the long term. We may be willing to lose battles as long as we move faithfully forward to win the war.

No need to be a martyr for some petty cause.

DON'T FRET OR REGRET—LET IT GO

When we have given something our best effort, when we have held our ground in the midst of the turbulence, when we have endured all we can, when it is time to rest and recuperate—then we must do so.

A friend of mine said, "I have a Savior; I don't need to be one." We are not the master of the universe. Never have been and never will be.

We need to do what is honest and just and then be settled with it.

These are terribly turbulent times. With all the stresses I identified at the beginning of this chapter, it is exhausting to even think about how unsettled our lives have become.

So we do our best and then we let go, retreat to our beds at night, and enjoy a peaceful sleep—all is in God's hands, thanks be to God.

Most of the real problems in the world are way too big for us humble folks to overcome. The best we can do is to play our part diligently and be thankful for the privilege. We work hard, my friends. We do our very best. We are diligent and faithful. Then we let go.

The tomb is empty! Grace abounds!

APPENDIX 1

PERSONAL ASSESSMENT

It is time to take stock and measure our ministries against the characteristics of codependence. To what extent do we have this disease ourselves? In what ways has it impacted our practice of ministry?[1]

Obviously, this exercise will only have merit if it is taken honestly without minimization, denial, or delusion. To have that courage born of grace will be helpful for this endeavor. Dare to be true and accurate in your responses. It will be liberating.

Personal Assessment

For each item, circle the response that most accurately defines your actions most of the time.

1. Have you lost sleep because of the behavior or comments of a member of your church?
   Never   Seldom   Sometimes   Often

2. Have you extracted one or more promises from a member of your church regarding their behavior?
   Never   Seldom   Sometimes   Often

3. Do many or most of your thoughts revolve around your church or problems caused by one or more church members?
   Never   Seldom   Sometimes   Often

4. Do you fail to follow through on some of your decisions because you are worried about how that choice might impact one or more members of your church?

Never   Seldom   Sometimes   Often

5. Has your attitude changed or fluctuated regarding one or more members of your church (e.g., alternating between love and anger or contempt and indifference)?

Never   Seldom   Sometimes   Often

6. Do you think everything would be okay if only a troublesome member of your church would control their behavior?

Never   Seldom   Sometimes   Often

7. Has your mood or behavior changed drastically as a result of a member of your church's mood or behavior?

Never   Seldom   Sometimes   Often

8. Do you feel guilty or responsible for the mood or behavior of a member of your church?

Never   Seldom   Sometimes   Often

9. Do you try to conceal or deny problems for, make excuses for, or protect a member of your church?

Never   Seldom   Sometimes   Often

10. Have you withdrawn from outside activities and friends because of worry or shame over the behavior of a member of your church?

Never   Seldom   Sometimes   Often

11. Have you withdrawn from outside activities and friends because you were too busy or too tired?

Never   Seldom   Sometimes   Often

12. Have you taken over responsibilities or duties that were formerly done by a member of your church or that you think a member of your church should do?
Never   Seldom   Sometimes   Often

13. Do you feel hopeless and defeated, like nothing you can do will improve the situation?
Never   Seldom   Sometimes   Often

14. Do you feel that you give more than you receive in relationships?
Never   Seldom   Sometimes   Often

15. Is it difficult for you to feel good about yourself when others are angry with or critical of you?
Never   Seldom   Sometimes   Often

16. Do you have difficulty expressing your feelings, especially anger, because of fear about how others will react?
Never   Seldom   Sometimes   Often

17. Do you say yes when you would like to say no, do things for others that you resent, or feel guilty when you say no to others?
Never   Seldom   Sometimes   Often

18. Do you try to appear cheerful even when you're hurting inside?
Never   Seldom   Sometimes   Often

19. Have you violated the privacy of others in order to check up on them (e.g., reading their mail, checking their email or voice mail)?
Never   Seldom   Sometimes   Often

20. Have you violated your own values in order to avoid conflict or feel accepted by or connected with the members of your church?
Never   Seldom   Sometimes   Often

21. Have you done many things for others that they could do for themselves because you enjoy feeling needed?
Never   Seldom   Sometimes   Often

22. Have you done many things for others that they could do for themselves because you think you can do it better than they will or you don't want to inconvenience them?
Never   Seldom   Sometimes   Often

23. Do you not tell others about your problems because you don't trust they will really care or understand and you don't like to bother them?
Never   Seldom   Sometimes   Often

24. Do you pride yourself in your ability to go without and to endure pain and hardship?
Never   Seldom   Sometimes   Often

25. Have you neglected your own responsibilities at the church or at home because of your worry about a member of your church?
Never   Seldom   Sometimes   Often

26. Have you been engaging in some behaviors (e.g., eating, working, drinking, having sex, gambling, spending) more than you feel comfortable with?
Never   Seldom   Sometimes   Often

27. Do you feel somewhat righteous or superior to the members of your church?
Never   Seldom   Sometimes   Often

28. Are you unhappy when your parishioner is unhappy or is behaving inappropriately?
Never   Seldom   Sometimes   Often

29. Has your relationship with one or more members of your church been affected by feelings of anger, fear, contempt, disappointment, or distrust?

    Never   *Seldom*   *Sometimes*   *Often*

30. Do you think that if the troublesome members of your church really liked you, they would stop their problematic behavior?

    Never   *Seldom*   *Sometimes*   *Often*

31. Do you feel if you could just try harder to be more pleasant, patient, fun, interesting, exciting, pastoral, or spiritual, the troublesome member of your church would stop their problematic behavior?

    Never   *Seldom*   *Sometimes*   *Often*

32. Are you afraid that other people blame you for the troublesome behavior of one or more members of your church?

    Never   *Seldom*   *Sometimes*   *Often*

33. Have you been physically or verbally abusive to a troublesome member of your church when angry or upset about that person's behavior?

    Never   *Seldom*   *Sometimes*   *Often*

34. Do you feel more like a parent than a church professional to one or more of your church members?

    Never   *Seldom*   *Sometimes*   *Often*

35. Do you feel forced to exert tight control over dwindling church finances with less and less success?

    Never   *Seldom*   *Sometimes*   *Often*

36. Have you lashed out at other church members because you were worried about or angry at one or more specific members of your church?

    Never   *Seldom*   *Sometimes*   *Often*

37. Do you feel shame for staying in the relationship and putting up with the troublesome behavior of one or more members of your church for so long but are afraid to resign?
Never   Seldom   Sometimes   Often

38. Do the members of your church accuse you of being too impatient, critical, or demanding?
Never   Seldom   Sometimes   Often

39. Do the members of your church accuse you of taking things too seriously?
Never   Seldom   Sometimes   Often

40. Do you make extra efforts to please the members of your church because it is very important that they accept you personally and won't reject you?
Never   Seldom   Sometimes   Often

* * *

Now tabulate your responses. How many Nevers, Seldoms, Sometimes, or Oftens do you have? The Nevers and Seldoms are good news. They suggest healthy boundaries and freedom from disease in those areas of your ministry.

However, attention needs to be paid to the Sometimes responses. Look at each one carefully and put together an action plan to avoid those problems/issues in the future. The Oftens require immediate attention. This is a declaration of unhealthy boundaries, enmeshment, and disease. I would strongly urge you to consult a qualified professional for assistance in those areas. You are in deep. Trying to change your behavior on your own will be very difficult. You have probably been doing these things for a long time, and they are most likely reflected in other parts of your life as well. To adequately and fully address these issues will be painful work. Don't do it alone! Give yourself the attention you deserve, the care and support to which you are entitled.

You are not only "fixing yourself"; you are making valuable corrections to the practice of your ministry. These are adjustments that will benefit everyone in your care. So do it for them if you find it challenging to do it for yourself.

"Grace threatens all my normalities"—thank God!

APPENDIX 2
STUDY GUIDES

I have provided the following three study guides to provide structured opportunities for study groups to really get into several parts of the book that are relevant to the participants. The first study guide is for clergy and other rostered church professionals. The second is for personnel (mutual ministry) committees and congregational governing boards (church councils). And the third is designed for last-year seminarians who would benefit from a review of these topics *before* they get into their own ministries.

Each study guide is designed to encompass four exercises. Each exercise has a biblical passage and a step-by-step structure. Do them in the sequence presented and dare to be open to your deepest understandings and revelations. The group needs to find four different times to do each exercise—for example, four Wednesday evenings in a row or something similar. A weekend retreat would also be a wonderful opportunity to use one of these study guides. Allow at least two hours per exercise. And I recommend that the group size be no less than four but no more than eight. The larger the group, the more time will be needed to allow each participant to share and receive feedback. I also strongly suggest that a qualified professional be engaged to lead the event. Who knows what might break open that will need careful attention to address?

Because of the personal exposure requested by these study guides, an atmosphere of trust and safety must be established. You may want to take some time at an earlier date to do some trust building and create an adequate level of rapport for the study guide exercise to have value.

Do not take this lightly. This is another way we protect ourselves from being heroes or martyrs.

Please use the study guides for your growth and enhancement. And have fun. Be open. Remember, you cannot cure what you refuse to diagnose.

Blessings to you all.

STUDY GUIDE FOR CLERGY AND OTHER CHURCH PROFESSIONALS

Exercise 1

1. Have someone read aloud Galatians 6:1–2 (bear one another's burdens). This is a text that calls us to a lifestyle of mutuality. Even Jesus did not journey through his ministry alone. At its very beginning, Jesus called others to journey with him.
2. Look at the codependency graph. In an honest appraisal, find where you are predominantly on that graph. (Note: You may be in different places with different groups. Be as specific as you can with as much detail as is needed and appropriate.) Share your self-appraisal with the group.
3. Ask for feedback from the others in the group. Do they recognize that pattern in you? What evidence have they seen that supports that appraisal? Complete the codependency Personal Assessment. What did you learn from that? Discuss the results with the group.
4. Ask for prayers and support from the others in the group so that you may have the courage to own this personal diagnosis and the inspiration to properly address it in a loving and forthright way.

Exercise 2

1. Have someone read aloud 1 Corinthians 12:12–31 (the many parts of one body). This text reminds us that each individual has personal value and their own gifts and talents.

2. Review the Myers-Briggs Type Indicator (MBTI) from chapter 3. As best you can, find your own temperament (Intuitive–Feeling [NF], Intuitive–Thinking [NT], Sensing–Judging [SJ], and Sensing–Perceiving [SP]). Review the literature so that you have a good appreciation of what that means in terms of strengths and weaknesses. Appreciate what the blending of varied gifts and talents can do for the church.

3. Ask for feedback from the group. Would they agree with your self-determined type? What evidence can they cite to support that? What problems arise for you as a result of your temperament?

4. Ask for the prayers and support of the group as you seek to own the gifts God has given you and avoid the pitfalls as well.

Exercise 3

1. Have someone read aloud 1 Peter 2:9–10 (called into "priesthood"; journey from darkness to light).

2. Review the material on the theory of oscillation. Make sure you understand the concept and its implications for ministry. How do the members of your congregation see you, your family, and so on? How do they respond to you, and what kind of expectations (fair or unfair) do they place upon you?

3. Reflect on how you respond to all these expectations and share your thoughts with the group. Ask for feedback. Do the individuals in the group agree with your insights or do they challenge them? Ask for evidence of their opinions.

4. Ask the members of the group for their prayers and support as you seek to embrace, in a healthy and humble way, the role of a holy person—weak and sinful as we all are.

Exercise 4

1. Have someone read aloud Luke 10:25–28 (God's call to integrate our entire selves—body, mind, and spirit—into the work of the kingdom).

2. Pulling together what you have learned from the first three exercises, now it is time to focus on the movement from whichever quadrant you are in on the codependency graph into quadrant I. For most of you (like me), this will entail a movement from quadrant IV. This calls for working on ourselves, not putting the blame on others.

3. Design a plan that is honest but not impossible for you to take some very real and concrete actions that will assist in the movement to quadrant I. What will you do differently? How will you implement this change? What kind of accountability will you structure to hold you to the task? Share this with the group and ask for guidance and advice. You may want to make a mutual accountability commitment with one or more group members to hold you to the work you have designed. I would recommend this kind of mutual support. Structure the commitment in some detail, such as how you will report to one another and with what frequency, what evidence of progress you will provide, and so on.

4. Close this final exercise with a period of prayer for yourself and for the others in the group. Use this as a dedication ceremony that will call upon God to bless your plans and aid you with the courage and commitment that will be so necessary to meet the challenge. The group may want to close with a hymn of confidence and trust in God's mercy to endure over all our human failures. End on a note of hope and confidence in the love and grace of God.

STUDY GUIDE FOR PERSONNEL COMMITTEES AND CONGREGATIONAL GOVERNING BOARDS

Exercise 1

1. Have someone read aloud Romans 12:3–8 (we are all members of one body). Reflect on what that means for the life of a congregation.

2. Review the section on codependent roles. In an honest and open way, determine how many of those roles are knowingly or inadvertently

placed upon the pastor and other church professionals. Identify them in as much detail as you can.

3. Discuss in the group whether you think this is fair and appropriate or unfair and detracting from the overall health and well-being of the congregation and its ministry. What does this do to the pastor and other church professionals? Does it encourage them or discourage them? Is it an asset or a liability?

4. Plan how you can address role expectations with the rest of the congregation. How can they be educated in a useful way that will enhance the work of God's kingdom?

Exercise 2

1. Have someone read aloud Romans 3:21–24 (all have sinned and fall short). What does this say about the pastor and other church professionals in your congregation? Do we expect a higher level of perfection from them than we do anyone else? Why or why not?

2. Review the material on the theory of oscillation. How does this apply to our expectations (fair or unfair) of the pastor and other church professionals? It is fully natural to think of them as holy people. That imposed stance has been around as long as civilization itself. Does that make it right?

3. If we were to accept the pastor and other church professionals as mere mortals called to fulfill a "holy role" rather than being "holy people," how would that change the way the congregation functions? Is it reasonable to place some kinds of expectations on those who are ordained that we do not place on those who are not ordained? If so, what are some examples? At what price?

4. Plan a way to educate the members of the congregation about this dynamic and how we can be more supportive of those who are ordained. What part would overt expressions of gratitude and appreciation play? How can these expressions of gratitude and appreciation become more regular and dependable?

Exercise 3

1. Have someone read aloud Romans 8:31–35, 37–39 (nothing can separate us from God's love). Is this something we *really believe* or hardly believe?

2. Turn to the material on the codependency graph. Review the four quadrants and the impact each has on the ministry of a congregation. In an honest assessment, in which quadrant is the pastor and other church professionals placed by most of the members of the congregation? How does that impact their ability to do ministry? How does it impact their personal and family lives? Review the material on the "vitality bucket." How does that factor into the picture?

3. Openly and honestly discuss your feelings about the expectations of the pastor and other church professionals. Are they treated fairly? Are they allowed to be real human beings? Are they permitted to set reasonable limits on their ministry so as to provide time for themselves and their families? Can they honestly express their feelings (especially feelings of frustration, disappointment, and even anger) within the congregation? Where do you think the pastor and other rostered professionals serving in your congregation would place themselves in the codependency graph?

4. Plan ways that ministry within your congregation can be a safe place—*physically*, *emotionally*, and *spiritually*—for the pastor and other church professionals. What needs to change? How can those changes take place? Who needs to take the lead? (Clue: it isn't the pastor or other church professionals.)

Exercise 4

1. Have someone read aloud Romans 12:2, 9–11 (do not be transformed by this world). How can we rise above all the pressures and attitudes that we find in our world? Some of these attitudes have gone on for generations—some as long as civilization itself. Is the church called to be a counterculture movement, challenging the pathology of our culture? If so, how can that happen?

2. In a group discussion, review what you learned in exercises 1, 2, and 3. How have these new learnings changed your understanding of ministry? Where *does* the "buck stop" currently in the life of the congregation—and where *should* the "buck stop" from now on? (Clue: not with one person but with the entire congregation as one united system.)

3. Discuss how all the necessary changes can take place in a fair and orderly way that does not upset the work of the congregation but rather sets a new tone, a new perspective on what it means to *belong* to a church. With membership comes responsibility. Everyone needs to share in the burden of success or failure of the ministry. The pastor and other church professionals have key roles, to be sure. But they cannot do it alone. That is absurd and unhealthy. It makes the whole congregation sick.

4. Plan a strategy that will engage as many in the congregation as possible to redefine roles. What is a reasonable expectation of the "resident holy person"? What are the responsibilities of all the members of the congregation? How can the burdens be more equally disbursed to yield maximum effort and ever-increasing success? Determine to set the congregation's vision on the work of God's kingdom and not the pleasure of the members. Why does this congregation exist at this time and in this place? Support one another as you embark on this wonderful transition. It will be hard work, but it will make your congregation's ministry healthier and far more effective. Enjoy!

STUDY GUIDE FOR FINAL-YEAR SEMINARIANS AND OTHERS PREPARING FOR MINISTRY

Exercise 1

1. Have someone real aloud Exodus 3:13–14 and Matthew 28:19–20 (when God announces God's name, at the same time, God sends . . .). Where is God sending you? Into what kind of ministry? What are your expectations and desires?

2. Review the section on the theory of oscillation. Is this what you expected, to be considered a holy person? If so, how so? If not, why not? Have you asked yourself, "What am I getting into?" Are you ready—physically, emotionally, spiritually?

3. Make a personal inventory of your weaknesses that will become all the more apparent in the ministry, especially in regard to parishioners' expectations. Can you identify the origin of these weaknesses, such as personality types (temperaments), family-of-origin patterns, and so on? How will you address this in the ministry?

4. Discuss in the group your personal inventory and ask for feedback. What have they observed that can assist you in the task? Do they see the same things or some other weaknesses of which you may not be aware? Be open to their observations without needing to defend. They don't have to be any more right or wrong than you are.

Exercise 2

1. Have someone read aloud 2 Corinthians 12:7 (thorn in the flesh). What do you think was Saint Paul's "thorn . . . in the flesh"?

2. Discuss the meaning of the phrase "You can't cure what you refuse to diagnose." How does that impact your preparations for ministry? What might you be hesitant to diagnose that may inhibit your functioning in ministry?

3. Discuss in the group the reality that no one is perfect and that we carry our imperfections into ministry. However, according to the theory of oscillation, our parishioners will not be patient with our imperfections. After all, we are holy people who have all the answers and can do things mere mortals cannot do. How will you react in that environment?

4. Ask the members of the group to pray for you (and for one another) as you seek a strategy to address in an open and honest way what you may want to "refuse to diagnose" and at the same time deal with the rather exorbitant expectations of the laity.

Exercise 3

1. Have someone read aloud Ephesians 4:11–12 (celebrate one another's differences and gifts). As a clergy or church professional, what gifts might you have that the laity don't have? (Careful: this is a trick question.)

2. Review the material on the codependency graph and the MBTI. The MBTI does a good job of illustrating our varied gifts and talents as well as preferences. From that basis, project the possible pitfalls in ministry that the codependency graph details for you.

3. Discuss in the group the methods of stretching and bridging you may need to employ. Seek others' advice and counsel.

4. Describe ways you can support one another as you embark on your ministry in light of the codependency graph.

Exercise 4

1. Have someone read aloud 1 Corinthians 11:23–26 (the Lord's Supper). This sacrament, along with baptism, provides clear demonstrations of God's endless mercy and grace. How important will these be to you in your ministry, and how will you demonstrate that importance?

2. Discuss chapter 12 on "Untrashing the Temple." Appreciating ourselves as whole people—body, mind, and spirit—is terribly important in ministry. If we fail to take proper care of any one of those three entities, it will impact the whole person. Assess the ways you currently "trash" yourself and devise ways you can prevent that in the future.

3. Share with the group your plan to take better care of yourself—body, mind, and spirit. With special attention to the dynamics of codependency, what strategies will you implement from the very beginning of your ministry? Given the cultural expectations that are working against just such a strategy, what will you need to put into place to ensure a greater degree of success?

4. Within the members of the group, make a commitment to do good self-care as you journey through your years of ministry. Ask for one or more members of the group to serve as an accountability resource as you will do for them. Describe in detail how that accountability will happen: the frequency of contacts, the style of reporting, the openness to corrective advice, the desire to continually grow and mature in the faith and in one's own self-care. End this last exercise with a prayerful service of commitment and dedication. You may want to sing a hymn of courage and triumph. Make the focus not your strength or fortitude but the dependable mercy and grace so freely given by God. Celebrate God's love. Venture forth in hope.

* * *

Blessings to you in your ministry!

NOTES

Preface to the Revised and Expanded Edition

1 Phyllis Tickle, *The Great Emergence: How Christianity Is Changing and Why* (Grand Rapids, MI: Baker Books, 2008).

2 Mark Chaves and Alison Eagle, *Clergy Compensation: National Trends and Local Realities*, Duke University, July 2016, https://tinyurl.com/yy8dzh56.

Chapter 1

1 Arch Hart, presentation given at Fuller Seminary, Glen Eyrie Conference Center, Colorado Springs, CO, November 7–10, 1991.

2 Michael Lowe Morris and Priscilla White Blanton, "The Influence of Work-Related Stressors on Clergy Husbands and Their Wives," *Family Relations* 43, no. 2 (April 1994): 189–95.

3 Becky R. McMillan, "The View from Pulpit and Pew: Provocative Findings on Pastoral Leadership in the 21st Century" (presentation, annual meeting of the Society for the Advancement of Continuing Education for Ministry, Lambuth Inn, Lake Junaluska, NC, February 21–24, 2003); Bob Wells, "Which Way to Clergy Health?," *Divinity*, Fall 2002.

Chapter 2

1 *Merriam-Webster*, s.v. "burnout," accessed July 21, 2021, https://www.merriam-webster.com/dictionary/burnout.

2 *Merriam-Webster*.

3 Gerald G. May, *Addiction and Grace* (San Francisco: Harper & Row, 1988), 9.

4 May, 38.

5 Anne Wilson Schaef, *Co-dependence: Misunderstood—Mistreated* (San Francisco: HarperSanFrancisco, 1986), 30.

Chapter 3

1 David Keirsey and Marilyn Bates, *Please Understand Me: Character and Temperament Types* (Del Mar, CA: Prometheus Nemesis, 1984).
2 Roy Oswald and Otto Kroeger, *Personality Types and Religious Leadership* (Lanham, MD: Alban Institute, 1988).
3 Schaef, *Co-dependence*, 44.
4 Schaef, 45.
5 Schaef, 51.

Chapter 4

1 Donald R. Hands and Wayne L. Fehr, *Spiritual Wholeness for Clergy: A New Psychology of Intimacy with God, Self, and Others* (Lanham, MD: Alban Institute, 1993), 35, 39.
2 Anne Wilson Schaef and Diane Fassel, *The Addictive Organization* (San Francisco: Harper & Row, 1988), 125.
3 Schaef and Fassel, 135.
4 Steven L. McKinley, *The Parboiled Pastor: The Joys and Pressures of Parish Ministry* (Minneapolis: Augsburg Books, 1998), 22–23.
5 McKinley, 65 (emphasis added).
6 McKinley, 7, 14.
7 Roy Oswald, personal communication with the author, ca. 2003.

Chapter 5

1 Bruce D. Reed, *The Dynamics of Religion: Process and Movement in Christian Churches* (London: Darton, Longman and Todd, 1978).
2 "12 Symptoms of Inner Peace," North Carolina Lawyer Assistance Program, July 7, 2014, https://www.nclap.org/12-symptoms-of-inner-peace/.
3 May, *Addiction and Grace*, 127.
4 Michael Crosby, *The Dysfunctional Church: Addiction and Codependency in the Family of Catholicism* (Notre Dame, IN: Ave Maria, 1991), 185.

Chapter 7

1 John Frederick Lehr, "Helping People Understand and Manage Their Stress: A Pastoral-Educational Approach" (DMin thesis, Drew University, Madison, NJ, 1982). Copyright 1982, revised 2006.

Chapter 8

1 Roy Oswald, *Clergy Self-Care: Finding a Balance for Effective Ministry* (Lanham, MD: Alban Institute, 1991).

2 May, *Addiction and Grace*, 14.

Chapter 10

1 Federation of State Medical Boards of the United States, *Federation Bulletin* (Washington, DC: Federation of State Medical Boards of the United States, 1992), 73.

2 Thomas G. Gutheil and Glen O. Gabbard, "The Concept of Boundaries in Clinical Practice: Theoretical and Risk-Management Dimensions," *American Journal of Psychiatry* 150 (1993): 188–96.

Chapter 11

1 Viktor E. Frankl, *Man's Search for Meaning: An Introduction to Logotherapy*, 4th ed., trans. Ilse Lasch (Boston: Beacon, 1992), part 1.

Chapter 13

1 Sarah Pulliam Bailey, "'I Feel So Distant from God': Popular D.C.-Area Pastor Confesses He's Tired, Announces Sabbatical," *Washington Post*, December 11, 2019, https://tinyurl.com/yxqzbyhr.

2 Chaves and Eagle, *Clergy Compensation*.

3 "In U.S., Decline of Christianity Continues at Rapid Pace," Pew Research Center, Religion and Public Life, October 17, 2019, https://tinyurl.com/y4ovyj5g.

4 Dwight Zscheile, "Will the ELCA Be Gone in 30 Years?," Faith+Leader, September 5, 2019, https://preview.tinyurl.com/y3yzgdhw.

5 Steven R. Covey, A. Roger Merrill, and Rebecca R. Merrill, *First Things First: To Live, to Love, to Learn, to Leave a Legacy*, rev. ed. (New York: Simon & Schuster, 2012).

Appendix 1

1 The original version of this assessment tool came from the Johnson Institute in Minneapolis. They did groundbreaking work in the field of interventions. And in addition, the Johnson Institute created an assessment tool for codependence. I have taken their work and revised it for the church setting. Validity and other scientific standards are not yet established for this instrument.